ADVANCE PRAISE

"Lawyerist.com spearheaded the movement to build a community of solo and small firm lawyers striving to revitalize and revamp the practice of law. In a shockingly short time, the community Lawyerist.com built and the ideas it nurtured turned my practice on its head—all for the better. The Lawyerist.com team has organized an overwhelming number of aspirations into actionable steps that any solo or small firm lawyer can implement to dramatically improve the running of their firm."

—MEGAN ZAVIEH, ZAVIEH LAW, GA; LAWYERIST
LAB MEMBER; GUEST ON *LAWYERIST*
PODCAST #110, #126, AND #164

"The team of Aaron Street, Sam Glover, Stephanie Everett, and Marshall Lichty are managing the amazing Lawyerist community that is not only helping small-firm lawyers nationwide learn how to be successful entrepreneurs, but making them enthusiastic about running their own businesses.

Twenty-five years ago, I left a large law firm to establish a solo immigration law practice. I had no business training and, consequently, I made a lot of mistakes in managing my practice. I've often thought that getting an MBA along with my law degree would have been pretty useful. Lawyer entrepreneurs today now have a pretty useful alternative to getting a business degree—Lawyerist. Whether it's attending their great conferences, joining one of its mastermind groups, getting one-on-one coaching, tuning in to its podcasts, consuming the fantastic content at Lawyerist.com—and now reading this book—today's lawyer entrepreneurs have the tools to become not just successful legal professionals, but successful business managers as well. Kudos to Aaron, Sam, Stephanie, and Marshall on this latest offering from Lawyerist."

—GREG SISKIND, SISKIND SUSSER, TN; AUTHOR
OF THE LAWYERS GUIDE TO MARKETING ON
THE INTERNET; LAWYERIST LAB MEMBER;
GUEST ON *LAWYERIST PODCAST* #94

"Far more than a business book, The Small Firm Roadmap is a sanity manual. Many, many entrepreneurial attorneys live with burnout, anxiety, addiction, and broken relationships. But that doesn't have to be the case. If you want to run a successful firm and maintain your personal well-being, this is the book to read."

—SHERRY WALLING, PHD, ENTREPRENEUR
PSYCHOLOGIST AT ZENFOUNDER, AUTHOR OF *THE
ENTREPRENEUR'S GUIDE TO KEEPING YOUR SH*T
TOGETHER*, GUEST ON *LAWYERIST PODCAST* #204

"*The Lawyerist community is where passion for law firm excellence meets intellectual horsepower. The Lawyerist has curated a group of extraordinary attorneys with bold notions for the future of the legal practice and provided a space for practitioners to not only share but enhance their ideas together. The Lawyerist team has uncovered and evaluated every business, wellness, and design-thinking resource to create a unique and invaluable perspective on how law firms do and will continue to thrive in the future. The Small Firm Roadmap is an absolute must-read. If you are just starting your practice, or you are simply frustrated with the archaic traditions of the law firms of yesterday and ache for a more modern experience, this is the book you have been waiting for.*"

—ERIN GERSTENZANG, EHG LAW FIRM, GA; LAWYERIST LAB MEMBER; GUEST ON *LAWYERIST PODCAST* #117

"*Everyone is always looking for 'the answer' for how to build a successful small firm, but nobody has had it, until now. This book is as close to 'the answer' as you will find. Spoiler alert: at the end you win big.*

The recipe for building a successful firm has been a closely held secret of a few brilliant lawyers. However, after years of working with hundreds of firms, the Lawyerist team explains the keys step by step in this first-of-its-kind book. This is a million-dollar read you can't afford to miss.

I read it. I did it. It works. This will be the new bible for law firms.

I've never been good at following roadmaps. But this Roadmap is one that every small firm lawyer can and should follow if you are serious about not just surviving but thriving in today's new legal economy. Read this book because it's best that you know how to drive toward success, otherwise you might wind up somewhere else."

—PATRICK PALACE, PALACE LAW, WA; FORMER PRESIDENT OF THE WASHINGTON STATE BAR ASSOCIATION; LAWYERIST LAB MEMBER; GUEST ON *LAWYERIST PODCAST* #91 AND #169

"*Lawyerist* is the essential online resource for twenty-first-century solo and small-firm lawyers in the United States. The Lawyerist team balances practical guidance about the business of law with forward-looking insight on legal technology and socially responsible advice for tomorrow's community-minded lawyer. If you want to know what the future of small-firm law looks like and how to get there, *The Small Firm Roadmap* should be your counsel of choice."

—JORDAN FURLONG, LAW21, AUTHOR OF *LAW IS A BUYER'S MARKET*, GUEST ON *LAWYERIST PODCAST* #124 AND #185

"For most lawyers, business + law = 'blaw,' or some other painfully disinterested noise they generate from their visceral depths. But it's not really disinterest, it's more akin to fear—fear that this lawyer can't be that businessperson. And that's crap. Business is just another collection of precedent and procedure that, once mastered, allows you to pursue business opportunities as deftly as legal ones. The Lawyerist folks understand this at their own visceral level—so much so that they decided to write a book about it. It's their 'summary judgement' from over ten-plus years of helping thousands of lawyers replace 'blaw' with action."

—MARK BRITTON, FOUNDER & FORMER CEO, AVVO. COM; GUEST ON *LAWYERIST PODCAST* #223

"It's incredibly difficult to be a solo/small firm lawyer (trust me, I know—I practiced in a three lawyer firm for years). As if tending to case research, filing requirements, court deadlines, and communications from opposing counsel wasn't enough, you need to take care of your clients' needs and wants as well! It would also be wonderful if you enjoyed what you were doing in the process—but is that even possible? How much easier would all of this be if you had a clear roadmap for focusing on the things that you didn't learn in law school, yet are crucial to the long-term success of your firm? Guess what—the team at Lawyerist has done the work for you. All you need to do is purchase, read, and implement the techniques in this book and you'll be well on your way to creating the law firm you've always wanted."

—JOEY COLEMAN, AUTHOR OF WSJ BESTSELLER NEVER LOSE A CUSTOMER AGAIN, GUEST ON *LAWYERIST PODCAST* #162

"In many ways, I've 'grown up' as a lawyer with Lawyerist—I remember when the platform launched not long after I cofounded a small firm, and have watched Lawyerist evolve into a tremendous resource for solo and small firm lawyers. I'm excited to see the Lawyerist folks share proven methods for building a fulfilling and sustainable practice through a holistic, client-centric focus with The Small Firm Roadmap. My twenty-plus years in practice affirms this approach!"

—PROFESSOR CAITLIN "CAT" MOON, DIRECTOR OF INNOVATION DESIGN, VANDERBILT LAW SCHOOL, GUEST ON *LAWYERIST PODCAST* #211

THE SMALL FIRM ROADMAP

— THE —

SMALL FIRM ROADMAP

A SURVIVAL GUIDE TO THE FUTURE OF YOUR LAW PRACTICE

Lawyerist

AARON STREET, SAM GLOVER,
STEPHANIE EVERETT, AND MARSHALL LICHTY

Lawyerist

THE SMALL FIRM ROADMAP

A Survival Guide to the Future of Your Law Practice

ISBN   978-1-5445-0481-0   *Hardcover*

         978-1-5445-0479-7   *Paperback*

         978-1-5445-0480-3   *Ebook*

For Kevin

CONTENTS

INTRODUCTION

WHAT DO YOU WANT OUT OF YOUR LAW PRACTICE?

Many lawyers we work with in our Lawyerist Lab program (we lovingly call them "Labsters") have set clear goals for their small firms and have figured out how to make their goals reality.

For instance, Megan wanted a solo practice, but she also wanted to be able to take regular vacations without putting her practice on hold every time. To make that happen, she built a thoughtful, hardworking team around her. Now, even when she's on a four-week (!) European vacation with her family, she's able to come back and pick up right where she left off.

When Erin started her own practice, she realized she

would no longer have the luxury of a large team behind her. But while she didn't have the resources to staff a full team, she *did* have the resources to adopt a few tech solutions. Soon, she had learned to automate all the work of signing up a new client with just the press of a few buttons to work as effectively as she had with a team.

For Emily, the challenge was to find a way to represent clients with limited means. By being proactive and considering her ideal clients' needs, she launched a series of client-friendly solutions—such as limited-scope representation and payment plans. These days, her family law practice thrives entirely off flat fees. She offers clients a menu for every part of every case type. She knows *precisely* how much everything will cost and offers her clients the services they need at prices they can afford.

Lawyers like Megan, Erin, and Emily are paving the way for the future of law and of small-firm practice. But for every one of these success stories, there are twice as many stories of lawyers struggling to make their dream of successful small-firm ownership a reality.

Many lawyers are like Todd, who left his big-firm job to start his own practice. It didn't take him long to realize he had no model to build the kind of practice he wanted. Unsure how else to go about it, he essentially recreated the big-firm model and tried to graft it onto his small firm, unnecessarily adopting all the same expensive tools and resources that his former employer used. All this did was create a big monster to feed with tons of overhead and endless administrative responsibilities. Despite his best intentions, Todd had left himself no opportunity for the sort of creativity and openness he'd originally envisioned for his firm.

Many of the lawyers we work with have shared similar stories. Buoyed by visions of a practice where they can do things their way, where they can have more flexibility and control over their practice, these lawyers set out to create something uniquely their own. Along the way, however, the challenges begin to mount:

- Their work feels unending.
- The demands of both firm management and client work never stop.
- They're under constant stress, always feeling like there is more to do.
- They have trouble finding new clients. The phone rings all the time, but most can't afford their fee. It feels like every lawyer they know is competing for the same 10 percent of clients.
- They have problems hiring and retaining staff and associates.
- Associates they do hire just can't seem to live up to their standards, leaving them to redo everything.

No wonder so many small-firm owners feel stuck. On the one hand, they're overwhelmed and struggling to stay above water. On the other hand, they don't know how to get the help they need to relieve that burden. As a result, these lawyers end up feeling frustrated and alone. They believe in their vision and their ability as lawyers, but they just can't shake one single, inescapable fact.

They have no idea how to run a successful law firm.

THE PATH TO SMALL-FIRM PRACTICE

If you're reading this book, you've probably encountered struggles of your own on your way to setting up and sustaining your own small firm. While the details of your challenges are unique to your journey, we've found that most small-firm owners have a lot in common. For instance, the majority became small-firm owners by following one of a few common paths:

- **The Default Option.** You went to law school, didn't get the job you wanted when you graduated, and set up your small firm because you had little other choice.
- **Plan B.** After working at another firm for a while, you decided you'd rather have your own firm instead.
- **Entrepreneurship.** From the get-go, you've been

hungry to build and grow your own thing. As soon as you could, you launched your own practice.

- **Deliberately Self-Employed.** You might not be an entrepreneur, working to master the craft of growing a business, but you know you'd rather work for yourself than someone else.
- **Legacy.** Either your parent or your mentor owned a small firm, and you've always known it would be your path too.

However you came to small-firm ownership, we're willing to bet that it was no less filled with uncertainty and frustration. Uncertainty about its viability or desirability. Frustration over a system that often struggles to accommodate what you want to build and frustration over a culture that's stuck in the past and unwilling to experiment to better serve clients.

Perhaps most frustrating of all is that you know exactly what the problem is; you're just unsure how to move yourself or your profession forward.

The fact is, whether explicitly or implicitly, most lawyers are discouraged from directing their own careers. We're presented a narrow field of options, each with a preprogrammed path that we're expected to follow. Once we graduate, we're expected to either hitch our futures to a larger firm's wagon or start our own firm based on a traditional model.

Those choosing the latter option quickly face an important truth: we have little idea how to run a law firm, manage a business, market or sell professional services, bill clients, or earn a decent living.

Fortunately, there is a better way. You *can* own and build a thriving, client-centric law firm.

STANDARD SMALL-FIRM GOALS

Often when we ask lawyers what they want out of their practice, they state their goal in terms of clients, revenue, and billable hours. That's fine. But your goals can be so much more than that.

For some, their goal is working forty hours a week, not the sixty (or more) hours others often work. For others, it's about never having to choose between helping people and making money. For still others, it's about refusing to accept the model they've been given and creating a practice that works for *us* instead. These are reasonable, attainable goals that make us better at our jobs and create more fulfillment in our lives.

And yet, lawyers tend to think that these reasonable goals

don't apply to us—or at least they don't apply to us *right now*. Sure, they may *sound* like good ideas, but we'll worry about them later.

Your job is hard. We respect that. We respect that you have clients to serve and bills to pay. But the truth is, this mindset isn't doing any of us any good.

Look, we get it. We've each lived the lawyer trap ourselves and seen how damaging it can be for a healthy life. For each of us, there came a point in our legal career when we realized that the profession as it currently stands wasn't working for us.

For Aaron, it was seeing the huge disparity between two of his passions: business and law. An entrepreneur since he was a teenager, Aaron has a lifelong curiosity about growing good businesses. After graduating law school and entering the legal profession, he was frustrated by the disparity between the best practices of other businesses and the lack of business thinking in small law firms.

For Sam, it was the guilt he felt working from his laptop as he sat in the delivery room while waiting for his first daughter's birth. From that moment, he vowed to rethink the way he practiced law so that he could be fully present for his family when they needed him.

For Stephanie, it was the false choice between a career as a public interest lawyer or a career that actually made money. Resenting that choice but seeing no other option, she chose the latter. As this money-first mindset slowly began to consume her, she finally realized she could never truly escape her work. If she took off early on a Friday to enjoy herself for the day, the guilt of not billing would drive her right back to work on Sunday. Something had to change.

For Marshall, it was the slow realization that he could do more in the world. Being a good student had seen him through law school and landed him good jobs at successful firms. But despite his success, he wasn't satisfied. The firms he worked for were either ineffectively run or not set up for sustainable long-term success. Everywhere he turned, he saw a disordered system plagued with indifference and inefficiency. Convinced there was a better way, he set out to find it.

One by one, our paths led us to our work at Lawyerist. For over a decade, Lawyerist's mission has been to create a community centered around trailblazers like you to validate your work, help you refine your efforts, and share your story with others so they can learn from your journey and apply it to their own.

Driving this work is our belief in community. We believe

that the only way to create a new future for the legal profession is to build it together. Lawyers who surround themselves with mentors, coaches, and supportive peers will see this shared future and will work together to create it.

GETTING STARTED

We wrote this book to teach lawyers how to build successful, future-oriented, client-centered law firms. In solo firms and small practices across the country, lawyers are building a vision of the law that is empathetic, self-aware, and adaptable. This book will show you how to join this community and create a law practice that works for *you*.

This is not a book about how to build a law practice in the old model. The old model is broken. Instead, this book presents our vision for what a successful law practice *can be*. Whether you already manage a small firm or are considering starting one, this book offers you a path forward.

That said, this book is not a prescriptive, one-size-fits-all manual. There is no magic set of steps to implement in your firm that will guarantee success. This isn't a silver bullet. But it is a chance for a new beginning. *The Small Firm Roadmap* lays out a comprehensive set of tools and ideas you can implement in your own practice. But the details and execution of that process? Those are up to you.

Having the small firm of the future isn't about technology adoption. While it is important that you understand how to use modern tools, this is *not* a book about software tips. Nor is this a book about running a "cheap" practice. Finding cost-cutting opportunities can be great, but they are inconsequential if you're not focused on creating a client-centered experience and a sustainable, growing, and profitable business.

Finally, this book offers you the chance to build a practice that allows you to live the life you want and find joy in your profession. There is a lot of negativity and burnout in this industry, but it doesn't have to be that way.

Some of you may resist the ideas in this book or dismiss them as too good to be true. You may get through the first two or three chapters and decide that you'd rather stick with the status quo. And why not? After all, the status quo has worked fine for decades, right? Why shouldn't it work for you too?

Unfortunately, the status quo is no longer good enough. For reasons we will explore in part 1, the coming decade will see a perfect storm of social, economic, and technological changes that will profoundly affect how we do our jobs. In other words, change is coming whether we like it or not. We can resist this change and spend our entire careers playing catch-up, or we can use the Small

Firm Roadmap outlined in part 2 to become drivers of that change.

This isn't going to be easy. Change is often complicated and painful—especially for an institution as old and established as the legal profession. But change is *much more* painful when we aren't ready for it and don't understand it.

In the rest of this book, we'll help you find clarity about your personal and career goals as an owner of a small firm. We'll teach you the business and entrepreneurship skills you never learned in law school. We'll show you how to prepare for the coming disruptions in the legal industry. And we'll introduce you to a community of supportive peers and mentors who would love to help *you* create a better law practice.

─────── PART 1 ───────

HOW WE
GOT HERE

CHAPTER 1

LAWYERS ARE FALLING BEHIND

"If something in my practice doesn't change, I feel like I'm going to have a heart attack, die, and leave my two children without a mom."

These words stopped Stephanie in her tracks. Clearly this lawyer desperately needed help, and Stephanie knew she wasn't exaggerating. Stephanie had heard similar statements from other lawyers before. While many were more tempered—not every lawyer fears they might suffer a heart attack—lawyers across North America are unsure where their next dollar is going to come from. They're locked in an endless hustle, scrambling to unearth the next client and scrape together enough revenue to pay their bills. Or they feel general fear and anxiety about what an unknown future might hold for their practice.

In this environment, it's unsurprising that lawyers face higher rates of substance abuse, divorce, depression, and suicide than those in any other profession.[1] Of course, this isn't to say that *all* lawyers suffer from substance abuse problems and near-overwhelming anxiety. Many are simply stuck, overwhelmed, frustrated, or confused. They're getting by as best as they can, but they're unsure of their firm's long-term viability and have been so far unable to crack the code on sustainable growth and profitability. Being perpetually stuck in business is no way to live. And yet, most lawyers feel like they have no choice. They feel trapped in a model that leaves them with no choice but to put their heads down, push ahead, and hope their fortunes change for the better.

In a rapidly changing world, the modern lawyer is falling behind. What's more, those needing legal services aren't getting the representation they need, and the justice gap is only widening. Today, by some measures, a huge majority of people's legal needs go unmet.[2] Unless we as a profession find new ways to solve the access to justice gap, that problem will only get worse.

There is hope. While lawyers have fallen behind the rest of the business world, the opportunity exists for us to not only catch up but also to begin leading new solutions for

---

1   Report from the National Task Force on Lawyer Well-Being http://lawyerwellbeing.net/.

2   For more information, see: Legal Services Corporation. "2017 Justice Gap Report." 2017. https://www.lsc.gov/media-center/publications/2017-justice-gap-report.

the law's future. That is the core philosophy driving our work at Lawyerist. And it is this book's unifying theme.

To create a path forward, we must first take a long, honest look at the traditional law firm model and the many problems it creates—for lawyers *and* their clients. Once we understand the many challenges we face, we can adapt and build better law firms for the future.

THE OLD LAWYER-CENTRIC MODEL

For hundreds of years, lawyers have served as civic stewards, upholding justice and the rule of law. Law can be a truly noble profession. Lawyers can make a tremendous difference in their clients' lives. They can correct injustices, exonerate the innocent, and advocate for the sick, injured, and marginalized.

While lawyers remain critically important to civil society, the old model of practicing law is inherently lawyer-centric. The old model positions lawyers as elite professionals who are uniquely able to solve people's problems. This unique and elite status has encouraged lawyers to build firms centered around the whims and egos of lawyers. If you were a "non-lawyer"[3] working at a law firm, you were viewed as less important than

---

3   We hate the phrase "non-lawyer" to refer to people. Its current common usage in trying to emphasize that the only distinction that matters in law practice is between "lawyers" and "non-lawyers" demeans the important work that people in a wide array of roles play in law firms, the justice system, and the broader legal industry.

the lawyers in the firm. If you were a client of the firm, you interacted with the firm on the *lawyer's* terms. The lawyer decided when you were invited into their office. The lawyer decided when to communicate the status of your case. The lawyer dictated how much their services cost and how they accepted payment.

This model worked well enough for generations, even if it did result in society frequently thinking about lawyers through the lens of critical "lawyer jokes."

It turns out that the lawyer-centric professional firm model was never really a very strong business model. Because, in truth, most firm owners would prefer not to run a business at all—or at least they would prefer to make as few business decisions as possible. For reasons we're about to explore, the old, traditional law firm model simply doesn't incentivize them to.

NO TIME FOR LEADERSHIP

In traditional firms, the owner(s) is also the most profitable lawyer. When the product being sold is time, an owner's time is, therefore, the firm's most valuable resource. Since most firms still price the majority of their work on an hourly basis, this means that all value is calculated in terms of time.

In the eyes of any owner, then, every hour spent on strategy, systems, technology, accounting, management, pro bono work, creative problem solving, and hiring and mentoring employees is just an hour of lost revenue.

This mindset creates a sort of financial tunnel vision for firm owners: bill hours, get clients, and repeat. If they're not working on a case or out shaking hands at a networking event to generate new clients, they're wasting their time. The owner may be doing their job as a lawyer, but they're failing as the leader of their firm. This is a dangerous way to run a business.

LACK OF STRATEGY

Ask a firm owner about their business strategy and most lawyers will give you a blank stare. This isn't necessarily their fault. While law school may do an excellent job of preparing students to think like lawyers, it doesn't prepare them to own or operate a thriving small business.

Make no mistake, a law firm *is* a business. Firm owners need to understand how to set long-term goals, define their market and strategy, and manage a team. Unfortunately, there are very few resources to help them out. So, without knowing any better, when it comes time to start their own firm, most lawyers simply default to what they saw their predecessors do or ask their similarly situated peers what they're doing.

UNCLEAR AND INEFFICIENT DECISION-MAKING

Most small firms are built on some form of multilawyer partnership. Every partner gets to debate and vote on firm decisions. This may sound like a good idea, but it often leads to a fraught and ineffective decision-making process.[4]

Say, for example, that the firm wants to rebrand. First, they have a designer draft several new logo options and choose some finalists to discuss. They then assemble the partners for a meeting, put the options on the table, and try to pick their favorite logo.

The partners likely approach this decision with a mixture of instincts, anecdotes, egos, and feelings. They try to make a strategic marketing decision as a committee—with no marketing experts in the room, no marketing data to drive the decision, and no single person in the firm accountable for marketing success. A decision like this almost always takes too long, goes off on tangents or long debates, wastes the time of the most expensive members of the firm, and rarely results in a clearly defined and successful strategy with firm-wide buy-in.

This may seem like a small example, but it reflects a larger problem in the average law firm's decision-making pro-

---

4   Bruce MacEwen. "David Maister on 'Unmanageable' Law Firms (That Would Be All of Them)." Adam Smith, Esq. April 13, 2006. https://adamsmithesq.com/2006/04/david_maister_0/

cess and general lack of organizational structure. The decision has been made, but the decision-making process is poorly defined.

LACK OF CLEARLY DEFINED ROLES

When roles and process aren't clearly defined in the partner meeting, they often aren't well defined anywhere else in the firm, either. Organizational charts and clear accountability are a rarity in most law firms. And with or without a documented reporting structure, the hierarchy in a firm is rarely designed for clear management or decision-making accountability; often all the lawyers report to the most-senior partner, and all other staff report to a partner or an office manager who reports to the managing partner.

Most small law firms define team roles by status, not function. Small firms almost always have administrators, paralegals, associates, partners, and senior partners. Absent are their sales director, marketing director, director of services, or operations director, some of the first roles filled in most other businesses.

A system without clear functional roles and accountabilities makes it harder to lead clear strategies and make good decisions. It also means that management and delegation skills are lacking in firms without sound structure.

As a result, lawyers often end up unnecessarily siloed and overworked in their own firm.

LACK OF CLIENT-CENTERED SERVICES

What kind of service can clients expect to receive from a firm where the roles aren't defined, where one lawyer gets all the attention, and where the rest of the team is all but ignored? Indifferent, disjointed, and confusing all come to mind.

Lawyers working under the traditional model may be good at lawyering—that is, they create positive legal results by acting as fiduciaries and advocates for their clients. But, to be blunt, they often suck at providing those legal services in a way that's convenient or comprehensible for their clients. In many cases, people may rave about the *results*, but they rarely have anything positive to say about the experience itself.

Nor should they. As a profession, we often don't make things easy for our clients. We all know of lawyers who don't answer their phones, don't regularly respond to client inquiries, communicate by mail, and who only tell their clients the cost of their services at the end of each month and then demand payment by cash or check alone.

Lawyers could do much more to give clients a better experience. But historically, they've had no incentive to take a more client-centric approach. For reasons we'll explore in the next couple of chapters, that is changing. Today's clients live in the world of Uber, Netflix, and grocery delivery. In almost every aspect of their lives, they have the freedom to choose the exact service in the exact scope and style they want. Even the legal profession isn't immune to this change. If lawyers don't adapt to deliver exactly what their clients want (and need!), their clients will go somewhere else.

DISENGAGED ASSOCIATES

As author Jordan Furlong says, for many firms, their most valuable assets, their associates, walk out of the door every day—usually around eight o'clock or so, after most everyone else has gone home. Firm owners would be wise to protect those assets. But most firms use broken compensation models and offer little in the way of work-life balance. Their associates warm the seats in the office. These associates lack much incentive to stick around, and many decide to set out on their own.

At Lawyerist, we're all for lawyers striking out on their own to build their own firms. That's why we wrote this book. The issue is that striking out on your own doesn't always solve the problem. Once these associates leave for greener pastures, reality sets in: they have no idea how to get results, just like the bosses they left.

Every lawyer we know who sets out on their own is convinced that they can offer superior client-centered legal services while raking in the money and having loads of free time. Maybe one day they will—but not if they're operating under the same broken business model that their bosses were.

MARTYRDOM IS NOT A GOOD BUSINESS MODEL

The traditional law practice model is not doing enough to meet society's legal needs. It is also creating legions of unhealthy or overworked lawyers. We have become slaves to our profession, and far too many of us simply accept this as the way things are.

At Lawyerist, we know this path all too well. Each of us has lived it. We've filed TROs on Christmas Eve. We've billed nine hours a day while on vacation. *Two* of us even billed from the delivery room. Like you, we've worked ourselves into the ground for our firms and for our clients, and we've learned the hard way that the traditional model isn't doing anyone any good.

Every time he signed a new client, Sam would say, "*Your* problem is now *my* problem." Sam—and countless lawyers like him—want to reassure their clients and demonstrate how seriously they take their work. There's a difference, though, between reassuring a client you're committed to their case and living a life with no boundaries for yourself and your family.

If a system requires you to offer your every waking moment to your clients, to give them your personal cell number, and make yourself available morning, noon, and night, then that system is broken. For starters, we simply don't add much incremental value by making ourselves available 24/7. More importantly, we can't help our clients if the very nature of our work is slowly killing us by requiring us to be on all the time. Martyrdom, it turns out, is not a good business model.

MAKE THE CHOICE

We're sure that you are aware of the problems we've outlined in this chapter. Maybe you don't think things are quite as bad as we've made them sound, but when you look at the big picture, it's hard to deny that something is fundamentally wrong.

We're not saying that all lawyers are broken. Far from it. Nor are we saying that all law firms are broken. Our argument is that the lawyer-centric model increases the likelihood of brokenness. Very few truly benefit from this old system, but many cling to it anyway because it's all they know.

We can do better. We can build better firms. We can provide our clients with better services. We can live better lives free from the fear of dying of a stress-induced heart attack. And we can design firms to be better businesses. If each of us works to address these problems on a micro level, then we can positively impact our profession on the macro level.

We understand that none of this will be easy. Change never is—especially in a profession like law, which seems to actively resist all change. But here's the thing: the world has changed dramatically in the last twenty years or so, and it will only accelerate from here. Eventually, these changes *will* affect your ability to maintain your current practice and serve your clients. How you respond to this change is up to you. You can resist these changes and keep pursuing the traditional lawyer-centric model, or you can embrace the client-centric firm of the future and all the opportunities that come with it.

For the remainder of part 1, we will explore how coming social, economic, and technological changes will impact the legal profession. Then we will lay out our vision for what the small firm of the future might look like—and why it will thrive in the new customer-centric economy.

---------- **CHAPTER 2** ----------

A LOOK TOWARD THE FUTURE

Lawyers will argue until they're blue in the face about what the future of law holds. Sometimes the arguments border on science fiction—we're looking at you, fellow robot-lawyer enthusiasts.

To be sure, sometimes it's fun to wear our sci-fi hats and imagine the wildest things we can about law's future. At Team Lawyerist, we've had plenty of debates about the value of robot lawyers. Though delightful as thought exercises, these debates are rarely relevant to *practically* creating a future-proof law firm. The question is, in an uncertain and ever-shifting landscape, how can anyone reasonably predict exactly what's going to happen five years from now, let alone ten, twenty, or thirty?

Prediction of the future is not our goal here. More often than not, detailed predictions of the future are exercises in futility. But you don't have to look to the future to see the changes coming to the legal industry; just look at the present.

Take self-driving cars, for example. As of this writing, these high-tech vehicles still largely belong to the future, but they're putting down roots in the present. Electric cars with limited self-driving capabilities are already on the market, and fully self-driving cars may not be far behind. For us, these innovations are visible on the horizon. As a culture, we've begun to consider what the future of driving might look like for our society.

We see the same thing in law. Even today, companies like LegalZoom and other DIY platforms are upending pieces of some practice areas. Where every aspect of estate planning was once seen as a high-value service offered by established firms, now anyone can get online, click a few links, type in some information, and produce a set of basic estate planning documents. Now, whether people *should* use web-based legal solutions is another discussion altogether, but the reality is that they *are* available and people *are* buying them. At least in that limited use case, people are already buying lawyer replacements—and that's not going to change.

In this chapter, we'll explore changes already in progress that are likely to profoundly affect the future of law. Our goal isn't to tell you what *will* happen. We don't claim to see a future that others are blind to, nor do we have any interest in arguing what propositions will or won't come true (except the robot lawyers, which Aaron says he is 100 percent certain will definitely come true *eventually*).

Instead, our goal is simply to lay out the major trend lines and help you recognize that *some* sort of change is coming. The more practiced we are at anticipating possible futures, the better we can adapt to the inevitable changes.

When we can do that, we change our entire mindset from confronting challenge to embracing opportunity. Lawyers specializing in traffic law could feel threatened by the changes self-driving cars will bring to their practice when robot cars never again speed or run stop lights, or they could choose to embrace this changing environment and become trailblazers in the new practice areas these cars will create (like self-driving car liability law). Similarly, estate planners can lament the decline of the part of their practice being replaced by only DIY forms, or they can pivot to offer clients the kind of personal support and caring that the internet cannot (at least, not yet). The point is, for every practice area that loses relevance, it is likely new ones open up.

Your future success as a lawyer depends on your ability to pay attention to these trends, anticipate how they might affect your practice, and pivot toward opportunities in which you are better equipped to solve your clients' problems. By anticipating what's coming and building a better version of it, you get ahead.

Before we dive in, we do have one little caveat: in the introduction, we explicitly promised that this isn't a tech book. We mean it. This definitely isn't a tech book. Still, many of the coming changes *do* have to do with technological trends. We don't expect you to read this and become an expert in blockchain or VR, but we do hope that this discussion leaves you with a general familiarity with these trends.

With that caveat out of the way, let's talk about the future—starting with a discussion of the present and how we got here.

MARKETS TRANSITION TO CONSUMERS

In 2015 blogger and business consultant Ben Thompson introduced a concept he called *aggregation theory*. Thompson's theory helps explain and contextualize many of the internet and business trends of the early twenty-first century. The phenomenon Thompson describes applies to every corner of commerce, from products and services to content and education—and, yes, even to law.[5]

---

5   Ben Thompson. "Aggregation Theory." https://stratechery.com/2015/aggregation-theory/

Aggregation theory argues that as the internet democratized access to information, consumers now have near-absolute freedom to find and select the exact thing—be it a product, service, or piece of content—that they want. This completely upended the traditional model, which forced consumers to go through a middleman for access to all their wants and needs. Now "aggregators" allow consumers to find the things they want on free platforms that connect them directly with providers, cutting out the distributors who previously controlled those interactions. For example:

- If you wanted a ride from point A to point B, licensed taxi cabs were essentially your only option. You followed their terms—no matter how dirty the car or how rude the driver—or you didn't ride. Now, Lyft and Uber offer a more diverse transport system and give passengers their choice of drivers and cars.
- If you wanted to watch TV, your choices were limited by what was on when it was on. If you couldn't find something you wanted to watch, you either had to grit your teeth and suffer through it or simply get up and do something else. Services like Netflix and YouTube have changed the game by providing content on-demand—with the latter even allowing users to create their own.
- If you wanted to take a higher education course, you had to apply to a college, get accepted, pay significant

tuition, and sit in a lecture hall—all under the control of a university. Now you can sign up for college-level courses on Udacity or Coursera, sometimes for free, and get accredited higher education credentials from your home on your time.

No matter the industry, market forces now favor companies focused exclusively on providing consumers what they want, when they want it, and delivered through an optimized client experience. Buyers no longer have to settle for the few poor options previously available to them.

CONSUMER SHIFTS IN LAW

This shift impacts law in two fundamental ways:

- **More informed decisions:** Any potential client can get on Google, Avvo, or Yelp, find whatever subset of lawyers they're looking for, research the differences between all of them, read about prior clients' experiences, dig into lawyers' biographies and social media reputations, and make a decision about the right lawyer for them—all before they actually interact with a single firm.
- **Lawyer alternatives:** Services like LegalZoom—and Google, for that matter—offer your potential clients a different route to solving their legal problem that

doesn't involve lawyers at all. Whether paying for a semicustom form through a DIY platform, or just downloading a PDF template they find in Google, they can customize legal documents to solve their problems for little to no money and at their convenience. Are these the best solutions to their problems? Rarely. But from their perspective, they now have the employment contract, LLC charter, or real estate transfer solution they need.

Either option puts the power in the buyer's hands. When people can literally summon a car to their doorstep with minimal effort, they're going to expect the same kind of positive experience when it comes to solving their legal challenges. If they don't want to play phone tag or navigate appointment schedules with an inconsiderate, unresponsive, or condescending lawyer, they don't have to. They are now beginning to have the ability to get the solution they want from the place or person they want, on their terms.

WEB-BASED ALTERNATIVES

While we haven't quite entered the era of the robot lawyer, we are already in an era where sophisticated algorithms can help clients resolve some basic legal needs. Your particular practice area may be safe for now, but as soon as a DIY platform offers your would-be clients a more convenient service than a traditional lawyer, you may suddenly find demand for your services plummeting.

When people are presented with a choice, they most often choose the easiest and most convenient option. If that means not using a lawyer, then all the better. This may feel unfair, but it's important to recognize the opportunity here. As of this writing, platforms like LegalZoom are primarily "forms" services. They help people create a variety of legal documents, like nondisclosure agreements, estate plans, and limited liability company formation documents for clients in a hurry or on a budget.

These documents are effective to a point, and they're certainly legally enforceable. But—so far, anyway—the quality still isn't as good as what most flesh-and-blood lawyers produce. As lawyers, we can bemoan a future where people use DIY document services and watch as they continue to gain ground on us. Or we can differentiate ourselves, demonstrate our worth, and position ourselves at the top of the supply chain. Many lawyers we know have already found ways to create new business opportunities by fixing problems in those algorithm-generated contracts produced by their digital competitors.

The point in all of these examples is that viewing law through this new internet-driven lens reveals countless ways in which lawyers need to continue to adapt to being more consumer-centric and test new engagement and service-delivery models based on how consumers want to receive services.

THE FIVE MAJOR CHANGES THAT WILL IMPACT YOUR SMALL FIRM

As we see it, there are (at least) five major categories of societal changes happening today that will likely impact your firm in the future. To be sure, the future is still unwritten, and we can't know exactly how these shifts will ultimately play out. But while the possibility exists that some of these changes will be non-factors for you, it's a safe bet that at least a few of them will have a direct impact on your practice. Some of the changes we mention might feel like we're being alarmist, which isn't our goal. Our point is not to scare you or paint an apocalyptic future—we're actually very hopeful and optimistic about the future—but rather to make sure you're thinking about what *might* be coming next so you can have some plans to adapt and thrive in the face of coming change.

CHANGE #1: DEMOGRAPHICS

While right now most lawyers—especially firm leaders—are still white, male, and aging, that's not what the broader population actually looks like in the US or Canada and will be even less true in the next ten years.

As with most things to do with law, demographic change is slow in coming, but it is definitely coming. This demographic shift will come to firm leadership and employees, obviously, but also clients. The future of law practice is younger and much more diverse than it is now.

Diversity and inclusion is not just a passing fad; it is a recognition of reality. There is no likely future in which your firm—or any company—is successful while having mostly white men as leaders, employees, and clients. More women than men have been graduating from law school for years.[6] Nearly one-fifth of the population has a disability of some kind.[7] And white people will soon no longer make up a majority of the US population.[8] In a future where the population of clients and the population of lawyers are more diverse, law firms will need to embrace these changes to build their teams and serve their market of clients.

6   Elizabeth Olson. "Women Make Up Majority of US Law Students for First Time. *The New York Times*. December 16, 2016. https://www.nytimes.com/2016/12/16/business/dealbook/women-majority-of-us-law-students-first-time.html

7   United States Census Bureau. "Nearly 1 in 5 People Have a Disability in the US." Census Bureau Reports. July 25, 2012. https://www.census.gov/newsroom/releases/archives/miscellaneous/cb12-134.html

8   William H. Frey. "The US Will Become 'Minority White' in 2045, Census Projects." Brookings. March 14, 2018. https://www.brookings.edu/blog/the-avenue/2018/03/14/the-us-will-become-minority-white-in-2045-census-projects/

CHANGE #2 ECONOMIC DISRUPTION

Sam and Aaron started Lawyerist in 2009 in the midst of the Great Recession. That global macroeconomic disruption and its impacts on small-firm law practice at the time were key motivators in how and why we started this company.

As we write this book in the summer of 2019, the United States is in the midst of the longest recession-free period in our country's history. We have no crystal ball to predict when the next economic downturn will arrive or how severe it will be, but based on 250-year averages, we're way overdue.

If the recession of a decade ago is any guide, an upcoming economic downturn would likely have major effects on clients, law schools, bar associations, legal employment, and our firms. It's worth thinking about how ready each of our businesses is for changes in the economic climate.

CHANGE #3: CLIMATE CHANGE

In addition to upcoming changes to our economic climate, we're also facing changes to our environmental climate. Already, almost yearly, we are seeing record-setting swings in temperature, drought, forest fires, and hurricanes. Extreme disasters are becoming almost commonplace.

How might this affect the legal profession? First, it could impact some practice areas. With more climate-related disasters, more people than ever need protection from insurance fraud, representation for catastrophic injury and loss, and so on.

Second, climate change will influence where people live and how they get to work. Changes in ocean levels could fundamentally change the landscape of our coastal cities and states. What if Manhattan or New Orleans become partially, but permanently, submerged? What happens if Florida is brutalized by Category 4 and 5 hurricanes every summer? If you're a lawyer practicing in these locales, how does this affect your practice?

Some of it is already happening. As we write this book, three of the four of us live in Minnesota, which experienced a record-setting-cold winter that kept people mostly inside for weeks at a time, including a record number of cold-weather emergencies that closed schools and businesses. With no other choice, employees in all sectors logged many of their hours from home or were forced to miss work. What if an extra-cold winter is the new normal? What if it's impossible to get to work consistently *every* winter where we live? There are plenty of solutions to this, including trends around productive remote work, but if we aren't ready for it and it keeps happening, businesses could be stuck.

At some point, we might stop treating extreme weather as exceptional and instead accept some of it as a new normal. You can either get ahead of this trend, or you can wait until the water is literally at your door.

CHANGE #4: THE NATURE OF EMPLOYMENT

The very nature of work has changed drastically in the twenty-first century. Employees in many sectors—including law—can work remotely while enjoying flexible hours, various life and well-being programs, and progressive forms of compensation. Everyone wants to be rewarded, acknowledged, and recognized for the work they do, and organizations across the board are working to create an environment that is more diverse, supportive, and accommodating to their employees.

Additionally, the nature of jobs themselves is changing. Trends in temporary, freelance, and gig work continue. Long-term employment with a single employer continues to become rarer and rarer as employees now routinely move between jobs every few years. Changes in and needs for specialization in technology, marketing, and customer service mean many workers need more lifelong professional training and education than they've needed before. The ability to work from anywhere—including having whole companies or teams who don't share an office—is a growing trend.

And whether we end up with *robot lawyers* or not, technological advances will almost certainly change the way we approach our work in the future.

These forces fundamentally change much of the nature of jobs and employment. This creates interesting possibilities for shrewd firm owners. It's easy to envision small firms in the future that are able to grow and shrink their businesses on-demand using the many remote, freelance-based resources available to them, depending on their current client load.

CHANGE #5: ARTIFICIAL INTELLIGENCE AND EXPONENTIAL TECHNOLOGIES

At this point, we are about 10 percent of the way through this book, and we've already mentioned "robot lawyers" a half-dozen times. So naturally, our section on the future of artificial intelligence is where we should talk about robots, but instead, we're going to talk about progress. We can't say what the state of technology will be five, ten, or twenty years from now; we *can* say with certainty that computers will be enormously smarter and more powerful.

Artificial intelligence has become a buzzword across almost every industry. At this moment, it is still more buzz than substance. But limited artificial intelligence technologies do exist, and they're getting incrementally (or exponentially) better all the time. Machines are now routinely beating the best human minds at chess, *Jeopardy,* reading X-rays and MRIs, and spotting keywords in huge stacks of documents. But despite the incredible sophistication of those artificial intelligence systems, they are still very narrowly trained for a specific task: a chess AI will beat a grandmaster at chess but can't beat your four-year-old at Candy Land.

So why all the hype? Simply put, because AI and other technologies have vast potential.

For the past half century, advancements in computer development have closely followed "Moore's Law[9]"—the 1965 prediction by Intel CEO Gordon Moore that the number of transistors on a microchip (and thus the power of computers) would double about every two years. The exponential growth of computing power in the last fifty years allowed for massive improvements in technology and the power of software and computers to continue improving at exponential rates has not yet run into limits.

Right now, advanced algorithms can perform many tasks quicker and more efficiently than humans can, but those same algorithms require constant feedback and testing.

---

9   Wikipedia. "Moore's Law." Accessed June 17, 2019. https://en.wikipedia.org/wiki/Moore%27s_law

A computer won't recognize an orange until someone teaches it to. But once taught, and with automated feedback loops built in to its processes, a machine-learning algorithm can get better and better and better in perpetuity.

AI won't be replacing lawyers any time soon. But it will help us take shortcuts. For instance, AI can help us categorize and understand hidden patterns in large data sets. This can be incredibly beneficial in those moments when your team needs to pore through massive amounts of information in a short time. Traditionally, a firm had to hire an army of contract lawyers to review documents for sixty hours a week. Now software can do some forms of document review faster, more accurately, and cheaper than any group of humans.

Consider Tesla and their line of internet-connected, somewhat-self-driving cars. As fascinating and impressive as they are, these cars also raise important safety questions. When a Tesla is involved in an accident, the details of that accident are transmitted to Tesla, which can then learn ways to prevent that type of accident in the future and push software updates to all other Tesla cars, instantly improving the safety of every Tesla on the road. Internet-connected, software-driven cars learn to get better all the time. When a Ford is in an accident, the other Fords on the road don't learn from that accident, and other drivers are just as likely to be in the same type of accident in the future. But a learning car fleet can improve, for everyone, constantly.

This same concept also powers digital lawyer alternatives like LegalZoom, which uses software algorithms to consistently find marginal optimizations and improvements to its documents. Though each learned change may be small collectively and building iteratively over time, these documents get better and better and better in perpetuity. So right now, their contracts have a way to go—a software-generated contract today is almost always inferior to one produced by an actual lawyer—but that won't be the case forever. While they might be half as good as you today, they could be 51 percent as good as you tomorrow and 300 percent better than you in five years. Without applying similar underlying technologies, your legal team cannot make the same improvements at the same pace.

But there is good news here. So what if lawyer alternatives are using algorithms and machine learning to their advantage? There's no rule that says lawyers can't do the same and find ways to start using tools to build software learning and algorithms into the work they do.

Emerging exponential technologies like AI, quantum computing, genetic engineering, and DNA analysis, blockchain and cryptocurrencies, augmented reality and virtual reality—and the exponentially faster speeds of 5G (and eventually 6G) internet that might power them—all have the potential to both improve and disrupt many facets of our lives.

At the moment, almost all of these technologies are in their infancy and their future paths are very unclear. But change is coming and some of it may feel a bit like science fiction. The point is not to sit back and wait for our robot-lawyer overlords or to deny that any of this is coming; the point is to get curious about the opportunities these changes may create for us.

Those opportunities may come in the form of improved DNA testing in criminal investigations, the development of blockchain-enabled "smart" contracts, global broadband access that allows poor and rural clients to meet with lawyers for video conferences, virtual-reality courtrooms, or more efficient AI-powered evidence analysis. Or maybe something else.

CHANGE IS COMING

Whether your particular practice will be more changed by demographics than by AI remains to be seen. Our point is not to send you down a sci-fi rabbit hole about how Bitcoin is going to lead to the downfall of all centralized governments or how virtual courtrooms will replace the need for criminal defense lawyers. Honestly, the far-flung, low-probability, long-term potential of these trends doesn't need to concern you very much. But it is important to care about what might be coming next, what some of the big trends might indicate for the direction things are headed, and some ways that you might be able to adapt as change inevitably arrives.

OF COURSE THERE WILL BE LAWYERS IN THE FUTURE

All of these changes have implications for law practice, but none of them spell the end of lawyers who are willing to learn and adapt. There will be more and stiffer competition from younger lawyers and lawyer alternatives. You will need to learn how new technologies work so you can help clients and courts understand how the law should apply to them.

Lawyers will thrive in the future if they are flexible problem solvers, not if they are human document assemblers. They will thrive if they can explain these changes to clients rather than being bewildered by them. Traditional law practice relies on the lack of change (and on lawyers' monopoly on providing legal services). Future law practice will be fueled by change.

Lawyers are still needed. Through years of training,

lawyers understand that solving legal problems can't be reduced to a training manual. Lawyers aggregate information and effectively deploy it using the right tools for the situation. It's about cutting through and getting to the signal. The more effectively and efficiently you do that, the better off your law practice will be.

Even in a changing and uncertain future, lawyers still have important value. But as a profession, we're falling behind. While alternatives continue to get better and better—with constant change and relentless iteration—we're treading water.

So what's the solution?

Demonstrate value to your clients. That's it. That's the big secret.

Today's prospective clients have many paths they can go down without ever having to work with a lawyer. Your job is to show them why you are the better alternative. Marketing, automation, and pricing are all part of this equation, but none of that matters if you're not demonstrating value.

Say you're an estate planning lawyer. If you think the value of what you do is the time you put into custom-drafting an estate plan, you're thinking about your value in the wrong way. You're competing with services, algorithms, and forms that currently beat you on time and will eventually beat you on quality too. For a typical estate planner, each new plan requires time and effort. For LegalZoom, the marginal cost of creating one more estate plan from an existing template is effectively zero.

This coming reality may seem dire, but you *do* have options:

- Go up-market. Create a more complicated estate plan and charge more for the service.
- Accept that there's more to estate planning than a template and build your business around other selling points, like superior customer service and client-centered content.
- Build your own software-enabled forms or services that also learn and improve over time but are also supplemented by an expert human to give clients the best of both worlds.

Whatever you choose, if you want to continue your estate planning practice, you will need to rethink your value and devise a new plan. Selling better hourly rate forms won't work as a compelling value proposition message. You'll need to do what the template cannot do.

So what does the law firm of the future look like? Our

examination of current trends helps us project how they might affect us in the future. But the truth is that we can't anticipate exactly what it will look like. And that's okay. It's more important to be aware of how the world is changing so we can change with it to better serve our clients.

We do know that learning to think like an innovative business owner—rather than like a "traditional lawyer"—will help you develop the tools you'll need to invent a future that works for you, your firm, and the people you serve. In the next chapter, we'll explore what thinking like a business means for your small firm.

CHAPTER 3

RETHINKING LAW AS A BUSINESS

With all the inevitable changes that we discussed in the last chapter, what will your firm look like five years from now? What about ten? Fifteen? How will you build your firm into a thriving business and take advantage of the many opportunities available to you as a small firm?

No doubt you have an idea, but perhaps you aren't clear on the details.

In this chapter, we will share our vision for the future of law practice and begin to lay out the roadmap that will help you make that vision a reality for your firm. While no two firms operate in the same way, we believe that the most successful firms share the following traits:

- They treat the firm like a business, not a traditional practice, and are clear on what kind of company they are trying to build.
- They are clear on their ideal clients, on what those clients most need, and on how to deliver legal services in ways those clients want.
- They leverage technology when it can save them time or improve the quality of their work.
- They stay ahead of the coming changes in ethics rules and bar regulations. They see the access-to-justice gap not as an unfortunate inevitability but rather as a problem to be solved—and a potential growth opportunity.

Running your practice as a business doesn't require you to reinvent the wheel. There is plenty of great information and advice about how to run a business. Here, we're simply reframing that information in the context of running a small law firm.

YOUR LAW FIRM IS A BUSINESS

It sometimes feels crazy to say as we write this in 2019, but we distinctly remember attending continuing legal education programs (CLEs) in 2009, back when Lawyerist was getting started, and getting yelled at for daring to claim that law firms were businesses. For some reason, a small, vocal minority of lawyers in our CLE audiences found the idea of their firms being seen as businesses as truly offensive. "We aren't businesses; we're professionals!"

Time for reality. Your firm is a business. Period.

There's a reason lawyers need to think of their firms as businesses. We need to think of our practice less as a vessel for delivering legal services, and more as a complete organization that has our clients' interests, employees' interests, and our own personal and financial interests in mind. Think of any "unicorn" company that's cropped up over the past several years, be it Lyft, Netflix, or Spotify. Each of these businesses has charted a different path to success, but at their core, they exhibit the following traits:

- They're forward-thinking, with a clear vision of the future they are trying to create.
- They listen to their community.
- They find creative ways to provide services and solutions to clients.
- They deliver value first and profit second.
- Their business decisions are thoughtful, data-driven, and efficient.

In other words, when we encourage you to think like a business, it's not so that you can exploit clients and employees for profits and cheap labor. Instead, it's so you can learn to take a more client-centered approach to your practice, learn to innovate, and become a leader in your community.

That's why many of us went to law school in the first place: to provide value, seek justice, and fight for truth and fairness. In the traditional law firm model, we tend to lose sight of that vision, but that doesn't have to be the case.

Lawyers are professionals by definition, tradition, and practice, but we are also business owners. But rather than see that as a burden, we at Lawyerist see it as an opportunity. When you approach both business and legal challenges in a more systematic way, you will win the future. In the process, you'll also be creating a firm that fits your goals and lifestyle—and that is focused on all the things that inspired you in the first place. In the next chapter, we'll explore the essential traits that will make that vision a reality.

THE DENTIST MODEL OF LAWYERING

Lawyers won't go away—at least, not in our lifetime—but we do believe the nature of lawyering *will* change, as well as the nature of how law firms are structured.

To get a sense of what that *might* look like, consider a typical visit to the dentist's office. First, the receptionist checks you in. Then, once you're seated, a hygienist enters and performs the majority of the work. Finally, the dentist pops in; looks over your charts, files, and X-rays; and then spends the next five minutes or so looking over your teeth and talking over your dental needs with you. If for any reason your dentist needs to spend more time with you, they will do so, but their work is structured so that they spend very little time with individual patients in for a check-up and no time at all on receptionist work or basic dental cleaning.

Dentistry may not have much to do with practicing law, but we can learn quite a bit from the way they structure their business. In an ideal law firm, the entire staff sees to a client's needs, not just a single lawyer. An administrative team sees to the client's practical needs, a paralegal sees to the important legwork of the client's case, and then the lawyer takes it from there, putting all their energy into the kind of work that only a lawyer can do.

We've seen the "dentist model" work to great effect. The trick is delineating specific roles so that everyone can care for the client in the way that they know best.

THE THREE HATS OF SMALL-FIRM LAWYERS

Too often, small-firm lawyers have worn a variety of hats without realizing it. In the future, successful firms will need to more clearly separate out the three different roles a lawyer can play in the firm:

- The visionary entrepreneur
- The firm manager
- The lawyer technician

Many small-firm lawyers, and all solo lawyers, are currently wearing all three of these hats, often without realizing they are distinct functions to play with distinct skillsets.

THE VISIONARY ENTREPRENEUR

It's obviously important for a law firm to deliver legal services, but it's also becoming more important for law firms to have a leader who anticipates how the job of delivering legal services will change over time. Slowly but surely, that person should confidently usher their team into the future. This can be a delicate dance, requiring a leader who is both forward-thinking and empathetic, someone who has a bold vision for the future of their firm but is careful to share that vision in a way that is empowering rather than terrifying.

As the owner of your firm, you are the de facto visionary of that firm.

While we hope you see this as exciting news, be aware

of the implications. As the visionary leader of your firm, much or your time will need to be spent not practicing law but rather collaborating with your team in an effort to design business and legal solutions for your clients.

The visionary firm owner of the future may not give up practicing law entirely, but a successful visionary will need to spend significant time dedicated to the visionary work of the firm.

THE FIRM MANAGER

Distinct from the visionary entrepreneur is the firm manager, managing partner, or COO. This person's job also isn't primarily to practice law, but rather to run the firm like a business to keep the machine running effectively. Their concern is less on imagining future solutions for the firm's clients, and instead on day-to-day firm management, operations, finance, and decision-making.

If you're the firm manager, then your job is to figure out how to implement a strategy to make the visionary's ideas a reality and to embrace coming changes in a way that supports and augments the existing performance of the firm. You're not concerned with adopting technology for technology's sake but rather with identifying solutions that help your business do what it does best: profitably provide legal solutions to your clients.

THE LAWYER TECHNICIAN

In a future lawyer/dentist model of practice, the law firm equivalent of a dentist is the lawyer technician. Unlike the visionary leader, this person is dedicated to effectively delivering legal services. Their time and energy are spent maximizing their legal work.

We often hear about solo and small-firm lawyers who tell us how much they hate the marketing, finance, and administrative work of their firm and want to "just practice law." For them, the role of a lawyer technician makes the best use of their interests since trying to serve simultaneously as a visionary or a manager often feels frustrating or overwhelming.

It's worth saying clearly: if you are best suited to be a lawyer technician, you may struggle as a true solo, which requires you to also wear the hats of visionary and manager to succeed. If your goal is to be the lawyer technician, then, we encourage you to give serious thought to finding law partners or employees who can fill those other roles or finding a firm you could join and have others take care of the visionary and management functions.

THE RISE OF FREELANCE LAWYERS

As the nature of employment continues to change and the gig economy grows, any company can grow or shrink both to meet short-term demand and to scale by hiring freelancers and contractors. In the future, many law firms may not even have partners and associates the way they used to. It's quite conceivable a firm could be owned by a visionary entrepreneur CEO, managed by a professional COO, and have its legal services delivered by staff attorneys supplemented with freelancers. It seems easy to predict the continued growth of legal and paralegal freelancers in the gig economy, which is already creating an entirely new career path in the legal industry. For some currently solo attorneys looking to focus less on business management and more on legal work, opportunities to become a freelancer will become more common.

STAYING AHEAD OF (OR HELPING LEAD) THE COMING CHANGES IN ETHICS RULES AND REGULATIONS

Quick disclaimer: This is not a book about ethics rules and regulations. Every lawyer has a duty to understand and follow the guidelines of their jurisdiction. Take time to learn what those rules are and how they apply to you.

With that disclaimer out of the way, let's talk about the world of ethics rules and regulations, and the coming changes to a traditionally rigid world. Slowly but surely, state bar associations, courts, and other governing bodies have begun to take a collective step back to reassess whether the current legal regulatory system is serving its purpose—namely, to help clients meet their legal needs through competent and ethical means. What they're finding is what many of us have known for quite some time: many of these rules have become dated, obsolete, or downright harmful.

First, consider rules surrounding the unauthorized practice of law. As of this writing—with the limited exception of Washington State's Limited License Legal Technicians ("LLLTs")—all states prevent "non-lawyers" from performing legal work. If these rules aren't already meaningless in the era of DIY document platforms, they likely won't hold up much longer. The reality is that lawyers are already competing with lawyer-alternatives in legal services whether they like it or not.

Similarly, right now, only lawyers are allowed to own law firms. In the coming years, that will likely change so that lawyers, law firm staff, and outside investors can all have equity in law firms. This means that, for the first time, firms could hire CEOs with no prior legal experience but with considerable experience in entrepreneurship and business management and give them equity as compensation. Such a change would likely have a ripple effect, bringing clarity to rules around marketing and advertising.

And make no mistake, the rules governing legal marketing are in desperate need of revision and clarity. For instance, consider how the Texas Bar Association reviews all legal advertising. Currently, lawyers are required to mail a VHS cassette (DVDs did recently become acceptable) to an advertising committee, which then reviews the ad and then determines whether it complies with their guidelines. This poses several impractical barriers to the modern lawyer, who has to find a blank VHS or a DVD burner, transfer their video to the long-outdated media, and then go through the process of physically mailing the package and then wait until a committee makes a decision about the contents of their video. In a world where anyone can send a secure link via Dropbox or other similar file-sharing services, such archaic requirements not only stifle innovation, entrepreneurship, and client-centered services, but they also don't really protect anyone from anything.

Inconvenient and archaic rules like this are bound to change eventually, but the fact that so many of these rules are on the books points to a larger problem for our profession: the widening gap between ethics and compliance.

The purpose of ethics guidelines is to protect clients against incompetence and fraud.

At this point, however, many of the regulations in the industry are centered around protecting the monopoly of the lawyer-only legal services model, not client or consumer protection.

This creates an environment of rules for rules' sake, and power for power's sake. In some jurisdictions, lawyers are required to send full legal disclaimers to their clients with every text message. We understand the intent of such a rule, but such extreme micromanaging of lawyer behavior helps no one.

Our aim is to return ethics rules and regulations to their core purpose, which is to protect clients from incompetence and fraud. Rules designed to protect a legal monopoly—such as those surrounding lawyer licensure, non-attorney ownership, and fee sharing—don't do that. While we strongly believe that lawyers are best-suited for providing certain legal solutions, we also understand that those solutions will be created regardless of whether the lawyer is there or not. For that reason, we don't believe in trying to protect lawyers but rather in teaching lawyers how to create the most ethical, client-friendly solutions.

The legal profession is slowly starting to move in that direction, but too slowly. So while we obviously encourage all lawyers to comply with the regulations of their jurisdiction, we also encourage you to question the efficacy of those rules. If outdated guidelines are preventing you from doing your job in the modern world, do what you can within the context of your practice to initiate change.

THE ACCESS-TO-JUSTICE GAP

Everyone who has a legal problem has that problem solved somehow. One person might reach a settlement or be acquitted for a crime, while another might go to jail or lose their kids. Whether a lawyer represents them, they represent themselves, or they get a default judgment for not responding, the issue will conclude in some way at some point.

The real question is: Are these problems getting solved effectively? Are these judgments for or against someone fair? The legal profession has been around for centuries, and yet in some states, as many as 80 percent of all people who use the court system aren't represented by lawyers.[10] No matter how much society progresses, no matter how much the world changes, for far too many people, their legal needs are going unmet.

At least part of this problem has to do with mindset. As a culture, we tend to assume that access to justice needs can be solved, or at least mitigated, by government and nonprofit assistance. This will never be enough. To close

---

10   Court Statistics Project. "Cases with Self-Represented Litigants (SRL). 2018." http://www.courtstatistics.org/Other-Pages/SRL_Main.aspx

the access to justice gap, we don't just need more lawyers engaging in traditional attorney/client representation. Lawyers are often expensive, inefficient, and no fun to work with. More lawyers are not the entire solution.

So what is the solution? Naturally, addressing such a complex problem requires a multipronged effort:

- Create a more accessible court system. The more accessible courts are, the more people can have their cases resolved without the need for legal assistance.
- Increase funding for public and nonprofit legal services.
- Modernize regulation and ethics rules to make representation of underserved communities easier through the use of technology and other lawyer-alternative solutions.
- Champion new law firm business models that address this issue in a way that is client-centric, scalable, and profitable.

For small-firm owners, this last option represents a tremendous growth opportunity, but seizing that opportunity means addressing the access to justice gap not as a legal problem but as a business problem.

COMMITTING TO SOLVING PROBLEMS EFFECTIVELY

People are solving legal problems one way or another on their own. As a lawyer, it's your job to understand *how* these legal problems are currently getting resolved, and then to build a business that can do a better job at solving them.

Naturally, there's no single solution. Some solutions revolve around court systems. Others revolve around funding for public and nonprofit activities. Others relate to regulation and ethics rules. By designing and running our firms as a profitable business, we can find new ways to innovate and find more solutions that work for more people—and in a way that's scalable to help others.

Being protectionist will not close the access to justice gap, nor will it help lawyers create profitable, healthy, and successful firms. Being protectionist will only preserve the status quo, which is *not* worth preserving. We want to recognize the reality of how the world is moving and what it'll take to solve the kinds of problems it will face.

Now that you understand how your law firm can operate as a business in this changing world, in the next chapter we'll identify the essential traits that will power your small firm to success.

CHAPTER 4

THE LAWYERIST VISION

There's something about lawyers, especially litigators, wanting to brand themselves as fighters—as bulldogs with boxing gloves. This mindset is deeply embedded in the legal community's psyche. As a group, we tend to look at competition for competition's sake. We like to argue. We want to debate. We want to win no matter what.

In many ways, this is the opposite of our vision.

We wrote this book to help *you* succeed in *your* goals, not to destroy the people around you. There's enough battle terminology in law already, and we aren't trying to add to it. Your goals don't have to be a zero-sum game against anybody else.

Every win doesn't require a loss. In fact, we don't even view winning as a competition. There can be more than one winner—and we can even help each other win together. That's what our Small Firm Roadmap, which we'll discuss at length in part 2, is all about: achieving your goals and getting what you want so that you and the communities you serve can thrive.

With that said, we do have one caveat. While our vision can work for firms of any size, from a true solo practice to a large multipartner firm, the latter is likely to have a tougher go of it. Big firms have had a great run. For decades, they've enjoyed a position of leadership and success in the legal community. The biggest firms got the best clients, had the most resources, and were well-positioned to dominate their market.

Now, however, it is our perspective that the old model of the big law firm is breaking. The opportunity is there for them to change, but when you're so large and so firmly entrenched in the old way of doing things, change can be difficult. Even the big firms that *do* have an eye to the future are at a disadvantage. They've grown so big, and they have so many moving parts and entrenched beliefs that by the time they see the writing on the wall, it may already be too late to evolve.

This isn't to say that we're rooting for the big firms to lose. Far from it. Again, we want every lawyer and law firm who operates responsibly and ethically to get their share of the pie.

For reasons we'll explore in this chapter, the future belongs to those firms who are nimble, forward-thinking, and technology enabled. More often than not, those are going to be small firms. To seize that future, the following considerations are essential to your firm's success.

TRAIT #1: INTENTIONAL

The second you decide to start your own law firm, you find yourself with two options.

1. Start your firm and hope all the details sort themselves out.
2. Intentionally design and create a business that serves you, your clients, and your team.

Historically, lawyers have favored the former, letting the cards fall where they may without putting any intention behind their actions. This is ironic, given that, by nature, we lawyers are trained to question authority. If we were trial lawyers and Albert Einstein was on the stand, we'd do everything we could to expose him as a fraud if it benefited our client. And yet strangely, when it comes to opening a firm, we happily toe the line.

Again, a lot of this has to do with our training. Law school prepares us to be amazing lawyers, not to be amazing business people. We aren't taught to consider the implications of owning a business. We may know exactly how to poke holes in a witness's argument, but we're lost when it comes to designing a business that works for our lifestyle, that generates money, that serves clients with empathy, or that creates a great work environment for employees. Without that knowledge, we simply follow precedent and copy the other firms who came before us, never asking whether there might be a better way to go about things.

To be clear, there is absolutely a better way to go about things. As we discussed in chapter 1, lawyers following the traditional model are literally killing themselves, increasing their risk for alcoholism, substance abuse, divorce, and suicide—all while struggling to make a modest living. The law firm of the future is many things, but above all, it is intentional. When it comes to setting up your business, we encourage you to check your assumptions and question authority. If precedent doesn't make sense to you, abandon it. There's nothing that says your law firm has to look like all the other firms that came before you.

TRAIT #2: ENTREPRENEURIAL

When we're practicing law, we lawyers have no problem

thinking creatively in order to create wins for our clients, but when it comes to our business, most new firm owners just copy and paste what has been done before. Instead of asking what they can do to make their firm great, they settle for mediocre and average, crowdsourced from the prior decisions of the other members of their bar association contact list.

If you're content simply to go to work every day and do your job, maybe you want to consider working for somebody else. Leading your own firm probably isn't in your long-term interest.

If you're in it for the long haul, take a moment to shake off that complacency and put on your entrepreneur hat. Here is your opportunity to do something truly amazing with your practice—and the more you invest in your business, the more you will get in return.

Entrepreneurs are focused on how their business works and how they can improve it over time to keep it going. This is a bit of a balancing act. On the one hand, it's essential that you establish and follow a set of rules and procedures. You need to consistently deliver high-quality legal service to your clients. On the other hand, you must also be willing to experiment if your firm isn't performing the way you expected it to and to adapt to future changes.

TRAIT #3: EMPATHETIC

We lawyers love to think that we put our clients first. After all, we're zealous advocates who take on complex legal problems on their behalf. That's all well and good, but in every other way, we tend to put our own needs ahead of our clients.

It's easy to forget sometimes, but being a client is unnerving. When clients interact with the typical lawyer, everything is a giant question mark: they don't know how much they have to pay, they don't understand the process, and they're afraid to ask questions for fear of contradicting their lawyer. Nobody wins in this scenario—and yet, unfortunately, this is the very environment many of us create simply by following the status quo.

It's not just common sense to want to offer a great client experience, but it's also good for your practice. There's plenty of data to suggest that improving the client experience leads to more business, happier clients, and fewer malpractice claims. In the medical industry, for instance, doctors with a good bedside manner are sued less. Companies that put an emphasis on the customer experience tend to perform better in the stock market. We're willing to bet that you too value client experience. The problem is that you were never taught to think much about it, let alone create it in your firm.

Let's talk about it now.

The empathetic law firm is the client-centric and employee-friendly law firm. Every system, every process, and every touchpoint must be designed around the people you serve, their needs, and their expectations.

Why is empathy so essential to the Lawyerist vision? Simply put, it humanizes your work. Any client—any person—no matter their legal need, should be greeted and treated kindly. If you treat your clients as an amorphous entity with a vague legal need, you won't be able to serve them to the best of your ability, as you will have lost all context for what they need.

Remember, when a client comes to you, the legal piece is likely only one part of a much bigger puzzle. Solving only for the legal component, then, won't solve their core problem. More likely, it will contribute to other problems down the road.

Representing clients with empathy means being able to step back and view the attorney/client relationship from multiple angles. Put yourself in their shoes. Be clear on what *their* goals are for their case, not yours. Then, ask yourself how you can solve these kinds of problems efficiently so that they are happy to pay and feel good working with you.

We'll get into all of this in part 2, but for right now, we'll wrap up this section by saying this: treating your clients with the respect and empathy they deserve begins with your employees. Design your business around people, and let that focus guide every aspect of your processes—from employee hiring and onboarding to client acquisition and services.

TRAIT #4: SELF-AWARE

Pop quiz: What's your favorite hobby?

Did you struggle to come up with an answer?

You're not alone. Lawyers are routinely overworked and unfulfilled. In all sizes of firms and all levels of the profession, they regularly work sixty hours a week or more. We sometimes forget that we exist outside of our law practice, and as a result, we start to lose our identity.

To invest in yourself and in your business, you also must invest in your own well-being. Those moments when you're *not* working are just as important as the moments when you are. This means allowing yourself to take vacations from time to time—and leaving your laptop behind when you do.

We'll be the first to admit that, on this count, it can be a little hard to practice what you preach. While we were writing this book, Aaron brought his work with him on a Disney cruise with his family. It wasn't until he saw the $90 a day internet package that he learned to let go and enjoy some well-earned time off.

Letting go may have been tough at first, but eventually it reaffirmed one of our core values at Lawyerist: to take care of others, you must also take care of yourself. Recognize what you need to live a happy life, and make sure your work supports it and supports you.

Another component of the self-aware lawyer is recognizing the role you need to play in this world without judgment. Are you meant to be the visionary entrepreneur? Are you meant to be the firm manager? Are you meant to be the legal services technician? Or maybe you're meant to be something else. Only you can answer that question. And a self-aware lawyer will answer that question for themselves with confidence and clarity and will do great things with whatever the path is for them.

TRAIT #5: ADAPTABLE

As previously discussed, the world is changing. We may not know exactly what the future looks like, but we're certain it won't look like the present.

Change is constant. What works for your firm one year may not work for it the next. Your job is to build a business that is adaptable. This doesn't mean surrendering to chaos. It means structuring your business in a way that allows you to anticipate coming changes, determine how they might impact your business, and respond in a structured and deliberate way.

TRAIT #6: TECH-ENABLED

A few years ago, a lawyer we know named Barbara was interested in starting a virtual practice. Unsure how to get started, she began investigating how other lawyers had created their virtual practices. Quickly, she realized (1) there weren't many out there, and (2) those that *were* out there weren't particularly successful.

Why was there such a low success rate? Aside from the virtual element, these law practices were completely traditional. The lawyers had simply invested in some software that enabled them to exchange documents over the internet and some other software to conduct phone and video calls online. Other than that, nothing else had changed.

That's not what innovation is all about.

Think of technology as a foundational tool. If adopting

tech is the only thing you change about your practice, then it won't get you anywhere. Technology by itself is not innovation. While it's sometimes difficult to innovate without technology, it's easy to *not* innovate *with* technology.

As Barbara learned from studying other virtual law firms, it wasn't enough to simply play with new tools and call it good. Playing was not the same as innovating. Barbara understood that virtual firm fundamentally broke the traditional model. To make it work, she would have to reconsider every aspect of her business—from her marketing strategies to her client experience.

When you're empowered and enabled by tech, you're also able to provide a more client-centered service. All good law firms are driven by their understanding of their data, which they use to make decisions about their business, make decisions on behalf of their clients, and answer client questions.

A client could ask you any number of questions:

- What's my risk on this case?
- What's my exposure on this case?
- What is my soon-to-be-ex-spouse likely to walk away from the divorce with?
- What are the prices that we can negotiate this contract for?

Answering these questions will always depend in part on a lawyer's skills, training, and experience. When it comes to representing your clients as human beings, the human element of the equation should play a role. But supplementing hard-earned expertise with the robust data sets offered by modern tech tools can help improve those decisions and lead to new and better strategies. This can help them decide which cases to consider or disregard, whether to take a plea deal, or what essential provisions to include in a contract.

Finally, smart tech adoption can also make your job better. For instance, you can be a highly skilled lawyer who is well-trained in researching and reviewing documents. But no matter how skilled you are, it's tedious work, and you're going to get tired and make mistakes. Software that is designed to find words or analyze concepts is going to be perfect every time—it can be trained to get better over time, can do more volume at faster speeds, and can do all of this without having to eat, sleep, or poop. This then frees you up to focus your attention on other aspects of running a firm that can't be reproduced by a machine.

We'll get more into the tech discussion in part 2. For now, just know that at least some tech adoption is essential for the firm of the future. Not only will it help you make your value proposition clear to your clients, but it will also help you automate your tasks and free up your time for more high-level business or legal matters.

THE BIG PICTURE

We believe there's power in finding your tribe and learning from each other. Right now, the number of small firms
starting to build the healthy practices of the future is still
depressingly small. But it's growing. Every day, more and
more lawyers find kindred spirits in the Lawyerist tribe
and support each other in building the practices they've
always wanted.

Too often, when lawyers try to innovate, they aren't
aware of the efforts of others around them. That's too
bad. The current legal system is pretty broken, with a
huge portion of legal needs going unmet. Somewhere,
there is a latent legal market just waiting for you to
serve them, but it's going to take some innovative thinking to find that market and help to close the access to
justice gap. To get different results, you have to think
differently about the problems facing underserved
communities.

Many firms have already begun to take those steps. By
adapting the business models, techniques, and practices
outlined in the past two chapters—and covered in detail
in part 2—these firms have found new ways to solve problems for underserved communities in a way that benefits
both parties and that is healthy and sustainable.

You can be one of those firms.

Before we show you how, there's just one more step. In order to win the future, you must first understand where you stand in the present. In the next chapter, you're in for a bit of a self-assessment, courtesy of our Small Firm Scorecard. Don't worry, no one's judging your results. This exercise is purely for your own insight—and, ultimately, your own benefit.

CHAPTER 5

INTRODUCING THE SMALL FIRM SCORECARD

After years of working with some of the most innovative small-firm lawyers in the world, we've come to a few clear realizations. First, many of the most innovative firms suffer from a set of the same challenges most small firms do: that even they never learned core small business management and entrepreneurial skills in law school. Second, we believe that there are a number of generalizable skills, systems, and practices that almost all healthy businesses have in common. And finally, that one of the most important things successful business owners share is clarity about their business goals and a confident vision of where the business will be in the future.

We wrote the Small Firm Scorecard so you can objectively understand where you *actually* are, not where you think you are. We guarantee you that you will have a different perspective of your firm by the end of this chapter.

HOW THE SMALL FIRM SCORECARD WORKS

This scorecard tests for the following core competencies, which we believe every small firm needs to succeed:

- Personal goals
- Business goals and strategy
- Client-centered services
- Client acquisition
- Systems and procedures
- Technology
- Finances
- People and staffing

By using this scorecard, not only will you have a better sense of where you currently stand, but you will also be able to develop an actionable checklist to design and create a sustainable business: your own Small Firm Roadmap.

HOW TO GET THE MOST VALUE FROM THE SCORECARD

Most of the lawyers we know are overachievers by nature. We designed this scorecard to appeal to your overachieving streak and to challenge you to move forward. You may not like the score you get (more on that in a second), but we hope you will see that score as an opportunity to improve.

Any lawyer knows how to work hard, do well, and beat problems. This is just another opportunity to do that. To maximize your success, we encourage you to keep the following things in mind.

DON'T GET OVERWHELMED

On the scorecard, you will likely learn a thing or two about you and your firm. You'll also likely notice a few areas that you never considered a problem but now suddenly stick out like a sore thumb. Those are normal responses and part of our intention behind this assessment. Not only is our scorecard designed to help you unlock a bunch of opportunity in the future but also to find some quick fixes to make right away.

BE OBJECTIVE

As you go through this exercise, be as objective and self-aware as you can. It's easy to want to give yourself perfect tens in every category across the board. But this isn't an exercise in ego. This is an opportunity to uncover the things that have probably been holding you back from the traction you've been looking for. If you've spent a lot of energy and care on one of these topics and really understand that you've got it, feel free to give yourself a high score. If you're not actually at that level, however, a fabricated score won't help you improve.

Remember, this is a qualitative self-assessment designed to help you and your firm seize the future. The only way to do that is to be reflective, thoughtful, and honest. If you don't know how to answer a question or aren't even sure what it's asking, that means you can't be doing well at it. Don't be afraid to give yourself a zero. This is a self-evaluation; nobody is deciding your score but you.

IT'S OKAY TO "FAIL"

Lots of lawyers, like us, are used to getting good grades. On this test, you might not. There's a very, very good chance you won't love your grade. In fact, you're likely to score in the C, D, or F range.

If you do get an F, we recognize this might be the first F you've ever received. That can be a tough pill to swallow. To be clear, we didn't write this test to make you feel bad—that's the last thing we want. If you feel a little upset after taking this test, here are a few things to keep in mind:

- **You're not alone.** Most of the lawyers and small firms

who take this scorecard for the first time get a D or an F.

· **Nobody's judging you.** If you take the print version of the scorecard in this book, nobody's even looking at your score. This is a tool for you to understand areas for improvement, not a judgment of who you are. Here's the key: lawyers have never had good opportunities to learn how to build sustainable businesses, so why would they expect to have built them without these resources?

Think of your grade as a baseline. This is where you are now, and knowing that will help you get to where you want to be. An F may not feel great, but it doesn't mean you're a failure. It simply means there's loads of opportunity ahead.

If you *do* get an A on our scorecard, then, first off, congratulations! That's not easy. Provided you gave honest, reflective, and thoughtful answers, then you probably have a successful practice with lots of happy clients. Our assumption is that you'll also be successful in the future.

READY FOR YOUR MOMENT OF TRUTH?

For your convenience, we've included our Small Firm Scorecard for you here. Please note, however, that the best way to take the scorecard is online. A couple reasons for this:

- You might need a different scorecard. If you are a true solo, then we have a different test for you, one dedicated to solo lawyers that removes questions about "teams" and "staff." The scorecard printed in this book is for firms of at least two people.
- Online is more convenient. Sometimes it's nice to put pen to paper. If you don't feel like tallying up your points and prefer instant results, then taking the test online is certainly your best option.
- Track your progress over time. If you take the scorecard online, we've built a dashboard so you can track your score and improvements over time. We recommend (and will send you gentle reminders) to retake it quarterly.

To access the scorecard online, please visit http://lawyerist.com/scorecard.

LAWYERIST SMALL FIRM SCORECARD

(Each question scored 0–10, results weighted to a 100-point scale.)

Instructions. For each of the following questions, rate your firm on a 10-point scale. If a word is subjective, like *reasonable*, define it based on your subjective value.

If you aren't sure whether we're using a word the way

you understand that word, use your own understanding. If you aren't sure what a term means, give yourself a 0 (and make a note to learn).

If you can answer yes to a question, give yourself at least a 7 even if you see room for improvement.

PERSONAL GOALS

1. Do you know specifically what you want to get out of your firm—how much money you want to take home, how many hours you want to work (including vacations), the kind of work you want to be doing, and the impact (if any) that you want your work to have in the world?
2. How close is your firm to getting you to those goals?
3. How confident are you that your firm will be able to get you to those goals in the next ten years?

BUSINESS GOALS AND STRATEGY

4. Our vision and values are clear, documented, and shared by all.
5. Our long-term goals are ambitious, important, clear, and shared by all.
6. We have clearly defined our ideal client(s) or the specific market of clients we want to serve, including a definition of who we aren't trying to serve.

7. We have a documented business model built around solving client problems in line with their expectations at an appropriate price.
8. We understand our ideal client's "journey map" from awareness of their legal problem to resolution based on input from actual clients and potential clients.
9. I have a mentor, coach, or mastermind group that challenges me and pushes me to succeed.
10. Everyone at our firm is working on projects and short-term goals that are connected to our long-term goals.
11. We use a set of key performance indicators (KPIs) to monitor the health of our firm and to help us predict our future success. Our KPIs are regularly updated and reported.
12. Our firm's leadership understands that management by consensus is not effective, so one person is accountable for each decision and for deciding based on data and our strategy.
13. Our firm occasionally conducts a competitive analysis and adjusts our strategy to win our market.

CLIENT-CENTERED SERVICES

14. Our prices, rates, or fees are designed around the goals and needs of our clients and benchmarked with our competitors.
15. We have systems in place to make sure we keep client diversity, access, and inclusion in mind.

16. We communicate with clients using methods they prefer, while following our data security needs.
17. We draft client communications and legal documents in a reader-centric way, with emphasis on plain language and readability.
18. We have a seamless intake, onboarding, and delivery experience for our clients that reflects the kind of client experience they want.
19. We have a process for capturing client feedback and know their level of satisfaction, and we actively work to ensure high satisfaction.

CLIENT ACQUISITION

20. Our firm's reputation in our community reflects the brand image we are trying to convey and the unique value we provide to clients.
21. We have a written marketing plan, and we use objective data to determine the success of our marketing activities.
22. We track our marketing efforts to potential clients, existing clients, former clients, and referral sources.
23. Our firm has a modern, mobile-responsive website that is focused on communicating our brand message. It has clear calls to action based on our marketing plan.
24. We use a variety of online and offline marketing activities to communicate our value in a way that resonates

with our target client market and is designed to convert them into leads to our firm.

25. We have a system for converting potential clients into paying clients.

SYSTEMS AND PROCEDURES

26. We have clear systems and procedures that reflect our core business model, and they are documented, understood, and followed by all.

27. We have clearly-defined systems for outlining and improving our firm's workflows and project management.

28. Everyone in our firm follows good personal productivity and time management practices.

TECHNOLOGY

29. We take advantage of technology when it can help us fulfill operational needs, streamline systems, help meet goals, and improve client service.

30. All members of our firm are trained in our systems. Everyone is technologically competent.

31. Our firm is paperless. (We scan and digitally file all paperwork, shred what we don't need, and keep anything we do need.)

32. Our firm is mobile. Everyone can use mobile technol-

ogy to work productively and securely from outside the office.

33. Our firm has conducted a data security threat assessment and has an up-to-date threat model and a written security policy.

34. Our technology systems reflect the security needs of our firm and our clients, and are used by all.

FINANCES

35. We track the firm's profitability and benchmark profit margins against our long-term goals and strategy, we have a plan for reinvesting in growth, and all firm leaders understand our finances and strategy.

36. We have access to sufficient capital and cash flows to fund our firm for the foreseeable future.

37. We have a written financial controls policy that describes how money is handled in the firm and who is authorized to make and approve expenditures.

38. We follow written budgets and regularly monitor consistent financial reports and financial KPIs.

39. Our invoicing, payments, and collections systems are focused on the payment preferences of our clients so they will pay their bills on time.

40. We have a written organizational chart that includes everyone in the firm and their actual reporting structure.

41. Our organizational chart and job duties (who does what) are structured to encourage employees to focus on what they can do best (their highest value) and to delegate other work to those who can do it better or more efficiently.

42. We hire, fire, onboard, and train people based on how they fit with our firm's mission and values and the roles in our organizational chart according to documented processes. We follow a "right people, right seats" model.

43. Our compensation and benefits structure for everyone at the firm is fair, rational, and focused on long-term incentives that reflect our values.

44. We have systems in place to make sure we staff our firm with diversity, access, and inclusion in mind.

45. Managers at our firm (anyone with direct reports in the organizational chart) are all skilled at managing other people, and we actively train them in the skills of people management.

46. Our firm has a culture that reflects our values.

47. Everyone is engaged in regular firm-wide and team meetings, and communication and feedback is frequent, open, and honest.

48. Everyone at our firm keeps the number of hours they

work in balance. Except in an actual emergency, no one in our firm regularly works more than fifty-five hours per week, and most work forty or less.

49. Everyone in our firm is allowed, and actually uses, a reasonable amount of vacation or paid time off.

50. Our firm has systems in place to support our staff with self-care, wellness, addiction-support, and mental health needs.

GRADING YOUR SMALL FIRM SCORECARD

Add up your 0–10 scores for each of the fifty questions. Compare your score of 0–500 to determine your grade below:

- **Grade F (0–299):** Most of these concepts were probably new to you or you just haven't taken the time to document and implement them. Let's find some time to get started outlining your roadmap and take the first step. If you know what you need to do but just aren't getting it done, you will likely benefit from an accountability coach. If you're feeling truly stuck, take time to work first on your goals in chapter 6.

- **Grade D (300–349):** You've made a little progress building some systems and procedures into your business but still have a lot left to do. It will be easy for us to help you prioritize some low-hanging fruit for you to move forward quickly.

- **Grade C (350-399):** Even though a grade of C might not feel like a big win, you are well on your way to long-term success. You will benefit most from taking the last remaining steps to improving your score and working with a community of others who are also moving forward.
- **Grade B (400-449):** You have done great work building your firm, structuring your business, and designing your services. You are on the verge of unlocking even more traction and will greatly benefit from a peer group of other forward-thinking firms.
- **Grade A (450-500):** Assuming you answered honestly, congratulations! You've implemented a number of sophisticated business management systems in your firm, have built your services around the needs of your clients, and have a firm that employees enjoy working for. As a rare firm on the cutting edge of our profession, one of the most valuable things for you will be finding a community of other advanced peers to support you in continuous improvement.

SEIZE THE FUTURE

We're hopeful this scorecard has given you a new perspective on your firm and provided clarity on what you can be doing to succeed. We're big believers in innovation and future thinking, but we're also big believers in taking care of your core needs first.

In part 2, we'll teach you how to create a foundation for your small firm that is both focused on near-term basics, and forward-thinking and future proof. While the scorecard may reveal that some areas need more work than others, we encourage you to work through each chapter in order to get a full sense of what your firm can become. Regardless of where you are starting, working with us to craft a roadmap for your firm will get you moving forward immediately.

PART 2

THE SMALL FIRM ROADMAP

CHAPTER 6

PERSONAL GOALS

The writer Don Herold once said, "Unhappiness is not knowing what we want and killing ourselves to get it." Herold might not have had lawyers in mind when he said that, but he might as well have.

So many lawyers we know have followed the same trajectory. As law students, their goal was to be generically awesome. Whatever they were told to be awesome at, they worked to be awesome at it. That's easy to do when being awesome means being a high achiever—getting good grades, winning awards, and passing the bar exam.

The problem is, when these same lawyers finish law school and strike out on their own, being awesome is no longer such a clear concept—there's no one around anymore to tell them what awesome is. Does awesome mean starting your own firm? Does it mean making the most money and owning the nicest things? Does it mean taking on high-profile cases or having the most client impact? Does it mean building a career that gives you the flexible home life you want?

When we don't have a clear idea of what awesome means to us personally, we default to what we think awesome means to others. This creates an unwinnable situation where the goal posts are always in motion. Does making a lot of money make us awesome, or is it winning the highest-profile cases? Could being awesome mean working for a nonprofit or in social justice?

With so much ambiguity, it's easy to feel unfulfilled, stuck between other people's expectations and our own—but unclear on what those expectations might be in either direction. It's like we're endlessly searching for something, but we have no idea what that something is.

No doubt you can think of a lawyer friend or two who fits this description. But what about you? Do you have clear-cut goals on what being awesome means to you? Do you feel like you're meeting those goals—and does meeting them bring you a sense of fulfillment?

If you're not sure, ask yourself the following questions:

- Do you know specifically what you want to get out of your firm?
- How much money do you want to make?
- How many hours do you want to work, including vacations?
- What kind of work do you want to be doing?
- What impact, if any, do you want your work to have on the world?

If you were unable to answer any of those questions, then consider this chapter your wake-up call. We believe that you can and *should* intentionally design the life you want to live. Your business should exist to serve you and allow you to achieve your personal vision. If it doesn't, or it won't in the future, what's the point?

In our opinion, not much. Before diving headfirst into opening your own law firm, it's important to consider what you want out of your practice. In this chapter, we'll discuss some key considerations when determining your own goals for your firm, and then we'll map out a step-by-step approach to establishing goals that work for *you*.

GETTING IN THE GOAL-SETTING MINDSET

Before we get into our conversation about goal-setting, it's important that we distinguish between goals and strategies. Each has its own distinct meaning and purpose, but the concepts are often confused. To keep it simple, *goals* are what you want to get out of your business, and *strategy* is the plan for *how* you'll meet your goals. Now that we're clear on that, let's talk about the different types of goals you might set in your life.

WHAT IS YOUR WHY?

To start clarifying your goals, let's start with your *why*.

Why do you do this work?

It's true that just about everyone needs to have an income and a job, but that can't be enough. If you have a small law firm only because you need a job, there's virtually no way you'll ever find a way to thrive. If your firm exists just out of default, there's no wonder things feel stuck and no wonder you don't have clarity on what needs to happen next. Also, if this is "just a job," there are lots of other ways to have a job without the stress, liability, and uncertainty that come from owning your own firm.

On the other hand, if you are clear about why you do this work, crafting clear long-term goals and building a successful strategy around them becomes much, much easier. Is your why about the change you want to make in the world? Is your why about having flexibility with when and where you work? Is your why about financial freedom or building wealth? Whatever the reason(s) you do this work, be as clear as you can about it. Write it down. And don't just write it down as an exercise in posterity, write it down as the core starting point for all the other decisions you make in setting goals, values, strategies, systems, and marketing campaigns. If you are clear on why you're building this firm, and actually mean it, then the decisions you make in crafting your firm should all flow directly from that, otherwise you are standing in your own way from achieving them.

RUN TOWARD GAIN, NOT JUST AWAY FROM PAIN

Often, lawyers who start their own law firms are running away from something. For example, they might be running away from their job at a big firm, which they hated. Or they might be running from another small firm that was poorly run. Or maybe they're running from working at a firm that overcharged clients relative to the services they provided and disenfranchised communities in need.

If you're considering starting your own firm, ask yourself: Am I running away from things I don't like or running toward things I love? It's great to know what you *don't* want in your practice, but don't let that consume your thought process. Once you've defined what you're running away from, take a moment to be clear on what you're running *toward* as well. If you don't take this step, you may find it difficult to build a firm that aligns with your goals for yourself, your business, and your clients.

BUSINESS VS. PERSONAL GOALS

Your business goals should align with your personal goals. After all, you need to make at least some money to live the life you want to live, whether that involves raising a family, working for a nonprofit, or arguing cases in the Supreme Court.

In that way, business goals and personal goals are intertwined, but they are distinctly their own and don't always impact each other. A healthy business life doesn't necessarily equal a healthy personal life. It's perfectly conceivable that someone could run a hugely effective small firm but be a lousy parent and spouse. Naturally, we hope that's not the case, but the point is that success in one set of goals doesn't necessarily guarantee success in another.

Depending on where you are in your life, your personal goals may be secondary to your business goals. Perhaps you're unmarried, uninterested in dating, and driven by the idea of building a successful practice. For many entrepreneurs, the internal satisfaction that comes from their professional goals is enough for them.

Alternatively, you could be more interested in designing

a practice focused on work-life harmony. Perhaps it's important for you to have a robust personal life, to travel more, to spend time with your kids, and so on. In that case, your business goals directly feed into your personal goals.

INTRINSIC VS. EXTRINSIC GOALS

Researchers have long been interested in the difference between intrinsic and extrinsic motivation. For much of our lives, we're driven by an extrinsic focus, driven to perform so that we can achieve some sort of outward goal. We read books so we can score well on a test. We exercise to look good. We clean the house so that it looks nice when visitors come over. We take on volunteer leadership opportunities to "pad our resumes" to impress parents, peers, admissions officers, future employers, or prospective clients.

Extrinsic goals are great, but we can't sacrifice intrinsic goals in the process. It's okay to read a book simply because you enjoy the storytelling or because you're just curious to learn what it has to say, to work out because it relieves stress or helps you live longer, or to clean the house because it helps bring a sense of order to your life.

If you spend your career working only for extrinsic reasons, you risk never feeling internally fulfilled. When considering your goals, you will greatly improve your chances for success if you're able to identify a set of intrinsic reasons for starting your law firm.

SMART GOALS

Now that you've begun to clarify why you're building your firm, what motivates you, what you want to achieve, and who you want to impact, let's turn your reasons into a set of documented goals. To make sure your goals are something you can objectively build toward and could even accomplish, they'll need to be SMART.

The SMART goal system—which stands for **S**pecific, **M**easurable, **A**ttainable, **R**elevant, **T**ime-bound—is nothing new. Anybody with access to the internet can search for information on SMART goals and how to apply them to just about any scenario. There's a reason SMART goals are so frequently discussed: they hold you accountable to your ideas and steer you away from the pie-in-the-sky goals that aren't actually attainable.

For instance, say your goal is to be the best criminal defense law firm in Tallahassee. That might sound good, but it isn't a SMART goal. For one, it's not very specific. What does it even mean to be the best criminal defense law firm in Tallahassee? Without a specific definition of "best," you will never know whether you actually accomplish the goal.

So let's approach it in a SMART way. On the second go-around, you chuck the "best in Tallahassee" goal and come up with something more specific: the top-rated criminal defense firm in Tallahassee on Yelp. Or the number-one ranking lawyer in Google for "Tallahassee criminal defense." Or to achieve an internal client-satisfaction "net promoter score" of 70. Any of those sound a lot clearer. Now, the question is whether it's attainable. When can you meet this goal? In six months? A year? Five years?

We could go on and on about SMART goals, but those are the basics. As you work to answer the questions in the following sections, use the SMART process to keep your goals grounded and actionable.

SETTING YOUR GOALS

A good set of goals is a bit of a balancing act. You must consider what you don't want along with what you do want, what your personal goals are relative to your business goals, and what intrinsically motivates you versus what extrinsically motivates you. With this understanding, you're well positioned to answer the following questions.

WHAT DO YOU WANT OUT OF YOUR LIFE?

This isn't exactly a self-improvement book. We aren't going to spend a whole lot of time on personal development activities, but we see personal goals as an essential condition for running an effective business.

The reason is motivation.

If you don't know your personal goals for your work, it will be impossible to have a clear motivation for improving your firm. There needs to be a reason to care about making hard decisions to change and improve your practice.

So, first, think about your current personal goals. Then, think about your current position, or perhaps the current state of your business. Are you confident that your current work situation will help you fulfill your personal goals this year? What about five years from now? Ten?

If you *are* confident that your current job will help you with your personal goals, we think that's great, but you're in the minority. Often, the lawyers we ask this question aren't able to answer because they never bothered to set personal goals to work toward.

If you fall into the latter category, here are some questions to help get you moving in the right direction.

- What brings you joy, meaning, and connection?
- Who do you want to have relationships with?
- How much time do you want to dedicate to those relationships?
- How will you nurture those relationships?

All of us work to find some kind of meaning in our lives, but *meaning* itself can have very different meanings for different people.

- What's meaningful to you?
- What do you want to accomplish in your career?
- How do you want to be known?
- What do you want to achieve?
- Do you want to impact your community?

Some people want to learn new things for the sake of learning.

- What do you want to learn in your life?
- Do you want to accomplish a goal?
- Do you want to go on an adventure? Run a marathon? Climb a mountain?

Now, let's turn our attention to joy.

- What gives you joy?

- What are you doing to nourish yourself, your body, and your spirit? What do you want to do?
- How are you attending to those areas?

Obviously, we don't want to neglect finances.

- How much money do you want to make?
- How much money do you *need* to make so that finances aren't a constant source of worry and frustration?

So many of the lawyers we speak to freely admit that they don't pay enough attention to the joy, meaning, and connection in their lives. It may not seem like it, but not setting personal goals is a big risk. In order to run a successful business, you must have some goal to work toward in your personal life.

Set your personal goals first. They don't have to be elaborate, either. Perhaps you want to take a vacation, spend a certain amount of time with your family, or have time to pursue a hobby. Once you have these answers, you can then use them to define your business goals.

HOW WILL YOUR PERSONAL GOALS IMPACT YOUR PROFESSIONAL LIFE?

Want to hear something shocking? Remember Megan,

from the beginning of the book, who takes a four-week vacation with her family every year? When she founded her practice, she identified vacation time as her primary personal goal. Starting with this goal, she then identified several other needs:

- She needed to earn enough to take so much time off.
- She needed latitude in her job to be absent for four weeks without damaging her business.
- Her kids needed a flexible school schedule if they were still going to get their education.

With her needs and clarity of purpose identified, she was then able to determine some business goals:

- Her business would need to automate certain tasks to reduce dependency on any one person.
- Her business would need support staff skilled enough to perform her duties while she was gone.

She was able to meet these goals because, in the early days of her firm, she had carefully thought out what she wanted and mapped out a path to making that happen.

The specifics of her story are her own. After all, personal goals are personal for a reason. Yours might not look anything like hers. They're up to the individual—or individuals—making up your firm. For every personal goal, identify a corresponding business goal, and then consider how to structure your business to make that goal a reality.

Setting business goals with partners or staff can get complicated, of course. The more other people are a part of your firm, the more you need to consider how your business meets *their* personal goals as well. Just because you want to take a four-week vacation doesn't mean that your partners will as well.

Especially for existing small firms that are just starting to answer these questions for the first time (or firms where one person starts answering these questions but others aren't), this can create some existential crises. What if your newly clear goals for your life and your firm no longer fit with your partner's? Is it time to break up the firm and start over? What if you now realize that you have an employee whose goals for their career aren't aligned with your goals for the firm? Do they need to leave? These are some of the hard questions that must be answered to move a firm forward with clarity for the future.

SHOULD YOU OWN YOUR OWN BUSINESS?

Being a business owner takes a lot of time, energy, and effort. When you own a business, you have to put in the work to find good people, train them, and then manage them. After you open your practice, you have to wear a number of different hats. You're no longer just an attorney. No matter the size of your firm, you're probably the CEO and maybe the CFO. If you're a true solo, you're also the collections department, VP of Sales, director of marketing, and the technology department. It's your responsibility to make sure that bills go out and bills get paid, to set the vision for your business, and to know what levers to pull to make your business operate.

HOW LAWYERIST DOES IT: PERSONAL GOALS

At Lawyerist, we're especially aware of this dynamic, and we do our best to help our team live their lives in the truest way possible while making sure that everyone on our team has personal goals in alignment with the work our company is doing.

Sam and Aaron have learned to spend a lot of open and vulnerable time together over the last ten years talking about their personal goals, how they relate to their goals for Lawyerist, and making sure those goals remain in alignment.

Sam, for instance, cares a lot about having flexibility in his schedule because it's important to him to pick up his kids from school, find time for his skateboarding hobby, and be with his family every day. Sometimes this desire for flexibility means he chooses to work less than full time. If he makes less money as a result, then that's fine with him. He also doesn't feel pressure if he has to stay home one day because we've created a structure and culture that encourages people to be honest about their personal goals. He also cares a lot about always having projects to work on that involve innovation, design, and creativity. This personal motivation of what he wants out of his work has helped Lawyerist resolve questions about Sam's role in the company and how we solve future business challenges.

Aaron, on the other hand, is a lifelong entrepreneur with a personal passion for learning how to build great businesses, spending time with other entrepreneurs, and generating wealth for his family. To align with his personal goals, Lawyerist spends a lot of time thinking about how to improve its own systems (just as it teaches lawyers how to improve theirs) and encourages Aaron to participate in entrepreneur peer groups that both support his personal goals and help Lawyerist uncover new opportunities for growth and improvement.

Sam and Aaron have different personal goals, but they have built a company that supports, rewards, and celebrates each other's personal goals.

This may sound idyllic, but it's easier to make it a reality than you might think. The trick is, if you want to be supported in living your best life, you have to decide what it means to live your best life, then decide what your firm needs to be to meet them, then communicate those goals openly with your team and make sure everyone is on board with the same plan.

Once you've mapped out your personal goals and considered how they might impact your professional goals, you'll have a very important question to answer next.

Think carefully about your life. Some people get excited at the prospect of owning their own law firm and wearing different hats. Others don't. If you fall into the latter category, maybe being a business owner isn't your calling.

There is a lot of mythology in law practice, and currently in the broader business world, that entrepreneurship and owning your own business or law firm are somehow inherently good and virtuous. This is just not true. Entrepreneurship is some mix of skill, passion, or calling, but it isn't for everyone, and that's okay. The reality is that owning a law firm isn't for everyone; in fact, it probably isn't even for *most* of the people who are currently doing it.

If you own a law firm and really want to be a business owner, that's great! But if you own a law firm are have realized that you don't really like the business part of your work, that you prefer just practicing law, it might be that firm ownership or management isn't for you. We hope you don't feel judgment or a sense of failure if that's true. In fact, we think that realization is probably one of the most important and valuable things you could do right now. Maybe reading this book, then, isn't to help you manage your firm better. Maybe it's to help you recognize it's time for you to work in someone else's business where you can focus on practicing law, or to hire a professional staff to change the nature of your firm-owner work.

It's important to realize what you want to do, how you want to spend your time, and what skills you want to master—especially since the skillset required to be an amazing attorney is far different from the skillset needed to be an amazing entrepreneur.

Just like it took you a lot of time to develop, hone, and perfect the skills necessary to become a lawyer, it will take you a lot of time to develop, hone, and perfect the skills necessary to become an entrepreneur. If that doesn't sound fun, just remember that you'll have to use those skills every day. Once you've started your firm, it's on you to put in the effort to hire, train, and mentor your staff.

Again, it's all about making sure you spend your time working toward your actual goals. There's no shame in preferring to be an employee. Just make sure you're employed by a firm that you actually like.

WHAT IMPACT DO YOU WANT YOUR FIRM TO HAVE IN YOUR COMMUNITY?

A good entrepreneur has a clear vision for how their business stands apart and benefits their community. What results do you want to have for your clients? What are other ways you could help your clients or your community that existing law firms aren't solving? In a world where a huge portion of access to justice needs go unmet, the ability for law firms to find new ways to solve legal problems in impactful but profitable ways are enormous. Entrepreneurial lawyers get really good at figuring out how to spot a gap in the market and then fill that gap with a unique, client-centered service. Unfortunately, very few firm owners think like entrepreneurs.

GET A QUICK WIN

In Tim Ferriss' popular book *The Four Hour Workweek* (no, we don't want you to try to run your law practice for four hours per week if you want it to succeed), he teaches some really valuable tools for goal-setting. Among them, he questions why so many people frame their retirement-planning and bucket-list creation along the lines of "once I'm finally retired, then I'll start doing these things I've always wanted to do." Tim makes the important point that we never know what our future might hold or how able we'll be when we finally retire, and therefore, we should find opportunities to pursue some of those "retirement goals" as soon as possible.

Whether it's a retirement or bucket-list goal, or just something you want out of your life, the surest way to get it is to make a plan for getting it now.

So if you've always wanted to someday take a month-long vacation to Europe or eventually be a parent who can coach soccer on Thursday nights, or if you think it'd be cool to get a yoga teacher certification, write it down, not as a ten-year goal but as a this-year goal, and start figuring out the details of what would actually be needed to make it happen.

Is it easy to find a way to take a four-week vacation? No. But if you put together a plan for what the trip's budget would actually be and how much you'd need to save up to pay for the trip and to cover some lost income and work with your team to plan out what it might look like for others to cover your work or for you to check in remotely each morning, or whatever it takes to make this happen, it probably can.

So map out one goal for yourself that if you achieved it in the next twelve months would feel like you were truly winning, then find a way to make it happen.

If you're following the Small Firm Roadmap, that means that, by design, you aren't starting another law firm that runs the same way other firms run. To chart your own path, you need clarity. Define your reason. Identify the impact you want to have for your clients and your community so that if you see a gap in the marketplace, you can be intentional in determining how your business can fill that gap.

ESCAPE THE "GENERICALLY AWESOME" TRAP

Only you can decide what awesomeness means to you. Unfortunately, most lawyers never make the effort. We don't consider what it would take for us to feel personally and professionally happy and successful. As a result, we work incredibly hard to achieve some vague something without knowing what that vague something is.

What happens? We never get there—but we're left exhausted from trying. We spend our lives working, working, working without getting any closer to what we're trying to achieve. For such little reward, being generically awesome sure is exhausting.

When you're clear on your goals, you're also clear on what *awesome* means to you. You have a vision, you have a purpose, and you have a direction. Perhaps those goals mean finding a spot in a firm that aligns with your values and lifestyle. Or perhaps those goals mean setting out on your own and charting a new path for your profession.

Are you now clear on your specific awesome? Great!

Now that you're on the path to more clarity on SMART personal goals and how they relate to your firm, your career, and what you're trying to do in the world, we can move on to how to use those goals as the basis for your firm's strategy and business model.

MORE RESOURCES

We've put together a set of free tools, templates, and worksheets designed to help you with your goal-setting process. You can download them at lawyerist. com/roadmap/resources.

CHAPTER 7

BUSINESS STRATEGY

Patrick and Ben joined Lawyerist Lab after five years in practice together. They dove into our business strategy training first. In doing so, they realized that their current firm seemed just like everyone else's and wasn't built to fulfill their personal or professional goals. For the first time, they gave themselves permission to explore new possibilities. In doing so, they realized they had a new vision for what they want to create.

They then set out to completely revamp their firm, including who they serve, how they serve them, what they offer, how they price it, and how they market. They realigned their team around this new strategy and built new systems and processes. Their firm is now headed in a totally different direction from where they started, now aligned with their personal goals, a clear set of ideal clients, and a model for delivering value to those clients.

Once *you* are clear on your personal goals and how they relate to the firm you're trying to build, it's time to start crafting a clear business strategy for how you'll achieve those goals.

A good business strategy consists of the following elements:

- Defined vision and values.
- Long-term goals that are ambitious, important, clear, and shared by all.
- Identification of your ideal clients and what they need.
- A documented business model.
- An awareness of current trends to leveraged to win your market.
- A set of specific, measurable key performance indicators (KPIs).
- A defined method of conducting a competitive analysis and determining market strategy.

If any of these concepts are new to you, don't worry. Once again, you're not alone. To most lawyers, the strategy conversation goes something like this: raise your rates, bill more hours, get more clients.

That may have worked at one point, but that's simply not enough anymore. Now that we've helped you identify your goals, the next step is to help you figure out a strategy to meet those goals.

ESTABLISH CLEAR VISION AND VALUES

We once worked with an attorney who was embarrassed to share his vision for his own law firm with the rest of his team. His reasoning? He didn't want to be laughed at for not achieving them.

Eventually, we convinced him that he was looking at the equation backward. If the people in his firm didn't understand what he was trying to build, how could they help him build it?

In our experience, this attorney's mindset is the norm. Most law firms do not openly share their vision and values, not even among their team. That's too bad. If no one knows what you stand for, then they won't know how to help you embody that vision, won't make a point of following those values, and might even act counter to them.

Do you really need a vision and values?

We think so.

That said, you don't need to make it a bigger deal than it needs to be. We're not asking you to take your team into the woods and practice trust falls (unless that's what you're in to). All we are asking you is to be clear on why you exist as a firm, what you want to do with your business, and what it looks like for someone to be aligned with those goals. And then document and share those values clearly and regularly with your team.

When we work with a firm, we can tell in a matter of minutes whether or not that firm has a clear direction.

One time, for instance, Stephanie worked to help a firm assess what was wrong and what they could do differently.

"What is the vision for your firm?" she asked.

The owner dismissed the question as "typical consultant vision talk." To him—and to many other lawyers we know—vision was all hocus pocus. He didn't think a vision statement could possibly help solve any of his business problems.

He couldn't have been more wrong.

As Stephanie interviewed the members of that firm, every employee said the same thing: They didn't know what they were doing, and they had little sense of what they were expected to be doing. One day, the firm was focused on healthcare regulatory work. The next day, they were focused on special needs trusts. No one knew what the change meant, nor did they understand how they were expected to pivot into the new practice area.

The owner may have dismissed Stephanie's question as mere "consultant speak," but everyone in his firm was begging for a sense of purpose and direction. With relatively little effort, he could have solved that problem, but he was unwilling to do so.

Think of your values as a living embodiment of the firm culture you're hoping to create, the approach to work you hope your team shares. They are the guardrails of your business, the north star guiding every decision you make—hiring, firing, employee reviews, client management, compensation, and so on. With so much riding on them, it's important that you take time to consider your values carefully. This isn't a matter of simply writing out an appealing-looking list, plastering it on your walls and website, and calling it good.

There are plenty of ways you can go about determining your values. Sometimes it works best to work from your own feelings and ideas. If you feel like you have a team that is clearly aligned with your goals, developing your firm's core values as a group project can work well.

However you approach it, be authentic to who you are. For most people, their values lie somewhere in their gut. They start as a hunch. They may change once you make them explicit and share them with others, but that's just part of the process.

To establish your vision and values, first your values must be able to point back to your business in a concrete way. If you set a vision and values that your firm can't work toward, then all you're doing is setting yourself up for a lot of hard conversations down the road.

Second, your values must have actual meaning. Vague concepts or aspirational ideals don't work well since they make it unclear whether or not someone is actually exhibiting them.

Finally, avoid "table stakes" values. Honesty, integrity, hard work, and doing your best are things that all good workers in all companies should always exhibit, they have nothing to do with your specific goals or what it means to work at your firm versus anywhere else.

Remember, the idea here is that these values should be the traits that drive your firm's specific culture and that, if exhibited, will mean that your team is aligned in pursuing your firm's goals in the way you want.

Once you've set your vision and values, share them. In our opinion, you can't share this information enough. Share them with your staff. Share them with your partners. Share them with your current and prospective clients. Share them with the world.

Just make sure you believe in them—and that you follow them.

HOW LAWYERIST DOES IT: CORE VALUES

The Lawyerist team is built around these six core values:

1. Build the tribe.

2. Improve the ecosystem.

3. Deliver value first and seek profit second.

4. Learn and teach.

5. Think inclusively.

6. Do great work that supports a great life.

At Lawyerist, we use our company's core values to inform strategic business decisions, such as launching new projects, testing new marketing messages, or even making the decision to write this book. We actively use our core values the most in the context of hiring and managing our team.

Case in point, when we post a job, our job postings spend more time talking about our core values and vision than they do discussing experience or education because we want only candidates who match our culture to apply. We care more that someone is a values fit for our team and our company than what college they went to or whether they have five versus seven years of experience. Then, during the interview process, we structure our conversations carefully to test whether that candidate might be a good fit. If someone doesn't match our vision of creating a supportive, sustainable,

---

people-focused business, they don't get any further in the process.

Even after they're hired, all our team members (and even our owners) are regularly held accountable to our values. Every quarter, we conduct reviews of everyone—bosses, peers, and direct reports on our organizational chart. We review each employee according to how well they fit our values and how they exhibit these values in their daily lives.

This might sound like a lot of work, but we've found that having and upholding clearly established values makes it easier to run our business and make decisions. Further, we've found repeatedly that our values offer a path forward when we're unsure where to head next.

YOUR FIRM'S LEADERSHIP STRUCTURE

At a firm one of us worked at as an associate, a legal assistant put in a request to take some earned time off for an upcoming family vacation. Following protocol, she submitted the request to the firm's partner committee and waited for a response.

Days went by. Then weeks. And still she'd heard nothing from the partners.

Meanwhile, her family was moving ahead with getting their vacation planned. They purchased airline tickets and made hotel reservations. They were excited for their trip but worried there was a chance the vacation request might be denied. That's a lot of stress to carry going into a vacation.

Finally, after weeks of waiting, the legal assistant built up the courage to check on the status of her request—worried there was a bad reason she hadn't heard yet and nervous to be seen as pestering her superiors as a junior employee.

She learned that despite the fact that no one responded, everyone had seen the email and was aware of the request. Individual partners told her they were happy for her to take the vacation, but they couldn't sign off on the request until they'd addressed it as a committee. When she asked when she could expect a decision, they said they didn't know.

Talk about feeling stuck!

Though she eventually went on her vacation, it shouldn't take five partners to sign off on a vacation request, and yet things like this happen regularly at many small firms.

The partnership committee is a management staple of the traditional law firm. It sounds like a good idea, especially when all the partners get along, but the reality is that it often does more harm than good. Here's why.

REASON #1: IT'S INEFFICIENT

Stephanie once sat in the offices of a large law firm while fourteen partners mulled which health insurance they should offer their employees in the coming year. Soliciting input is good, but eventually someone needs to make a decision. Committees of partners are famous for being able to analyze and debate options almost infinitely. And when lawyers are trained issue-spotters, they're often better at poking holes in the options presented to them than in picking the action to take. What's more, this creates problems for your decision-making process; when everybody's in charge of everything, nobody's actually in charge of anything.

REASON #2: DECISIONS COME LATE

Partner committees are famous for taking a long time to make decisions. Companies that sell things to law firms, whether it's malpractice insurance, practice management software, or marketing services have come to expect that lawyers have a uniquely long decision-making process. Frequently, these delayed decisions result in lost opportunities.

REASON #3: YOUR FIRM PLAYS IT TOO SAFE

Whenever a company takes a huge leap forward, that leap is often driven by a visionary willing to put the flag in the ground and make a bold bet on their company's future. Bold decisions are rare within a partner committee, since, by their very nature, they're designed to promote compromise. Frequently afraid to stick their neck out even a little just to get shot down by the group or have their ideas picked apart by overly critical partners, everyone on the committee eventually learns to play it safe, often resulting in lowest-common-denominator decisions for the company.

FINDING A BETTER FIRM LEADERSHIP STRUCTURE

Now, imagine a management structure where accountability is assigned to individual partners rather than a committee. In this scenario, you *know* marketing is your job. You're accountable for all the new clients that come through the door, and as a result, you monitor your client acquisition numbers like a hawk. The second you see something isn't going right, you're proactive, partnering with marketing staff to address a small issue before it becomes a bigger one. As the partner accountable for marketing, you know you have the authority to make the decisions you need to rapidly iterate and modify your plans and expenses to maximize the work you're doing.

If this sounds like idle fantasy, it's not. We've seen it in action—and it works. All it takes is a little attention to your business structure, and a little documentation.

CONSIDER A MORE-VERTICAL STRUCTURE

Most companies operate under a vertical decision-making structure. At the top is the CEO, who is ultimately responsible for all decision-making in the company but who does not make all decisions themselves. Moving down the ladder is the executive team, commonly referred to as the C-suite. Within that team, different executives are responsible for different functions—marketing, finance, human resources, and so on.

Historically, law firms have been the exception to that rule, operating instead under a flat governance model. One possible explanation is that firm owners tend not to see themselves as running a business, so they give little consideration to their governance model. Another explanation is in the way firms are founded; even if they eventually grow into something larger, firms generally start as small or solo practices. In such a situation, establishing a vertical decision-making structure might seem like overkill.

Even *small* businesses benefit from a CEO who guides and delegates the decision-making process. Further, in a vertical system, those with decision-making responsibility will see more opportunities to improve. When you know marketing is your responsibility, for instance, you will be more motivated to learn best practices and address problems, and others will know who to come to for marketing-related decisions.

DETERMINE FUNCTIONAL ROLES AND ACCOUNTABILITY

No one person has to be in charge of everything, but everything should have one person in charge. To keep your firm running like a business, you must design accountability into the system.

Organizational charts are helpful for this, allowing you to clearly see who is responsible for which areas in your firm. These are more than just a piece of paper that you pay lip service to. They're an opportunity to identify who ultimately owns decisions. This isn't to say that the accountable party must make every decision alone—input from other members is great—just that they have the authority to make a decision when it's theirs to make.

Different firms will have different organizational structures. If you're a solo lawyer with staff, for instance, most of the decisions *will* come from you. You might empower your staff to have their say, but ultimately accountability is on your shoulders, and you'll likely be wearing a number of different accountability hats. In that case, just make sure you know which hat you're wearing for any given decision and that your decisions are based on data and strategy.

If you're in a small firm with a partnership or a professional leadership staff, however, you can divide accountabilities.

For every decision that's made, someone should be in place to stand behind it. Dividing responsibilities often comes down to what the different members or partners are good at. For instance, one of you might excel at client-centered services, another might have a special interest in systems and processes, and still another might have training in finances. To keep everything running smoothly from the top, you'll have a single managing partner sitting as the CEO who sets the vision, tracks high-level work, and has ultimate accountability.

However you create your firm structure, the most important thing is that, if a decision is made poorly or isn't made at all, it should be clear where the accountability lies. This isn't to say that it's fair to run around blaming people—such behavior is antithetical in our philosophy—but it's important to hold people accountable for their decisions and use all the resources available to help them improve their efforts.

ESTABLISH KPIS

Once you've decided on your goals and set your firm's vision and values, it's time to think about key performance indicators (KPIs). These are the metrics you'll track regularly that are carefully tailored to measure how well you're doing the things you're trying to do. They help you track your successes, your failures, and important trends.

Put another way, KPIs are invaluable tools for better decision-making. By allowing you to see problems (and successes) more quickly, KPIs empower you to take action—brainstorming solutions, creating new goals and strategies, and redirecting your team's efforts.

The trick is knowing which data are important to track and which data are just noise in the channel.

Fortunately, there's plenty of literature out there that will tell you how to do exactly that, but before you go chasing all that information down a KPI rabbit hole, let's take a moment to categorize KPIs into a few general buckets.

- **Financial:** Examples include revenue, invoice amount, accounts receivable, budget expenses.
- **Marketing and business development:** Examples include your marketing funnel or sales pipeline, cost of acquiring a client, cost of delivering the service you sell, new leads who contact the firm, number of new clients per week, total number of clients.
- **Client satisfaction:** Examples include the speed with which you close cases and net promoter score.

So how might this play out? Say you acquire thirty fresh leads one month and only ten the next month. Given this scenario, it would be reasonable to predict that you'll only get a third of the new clients from month to month, since you only got a third of the intake. Sure, you might get lucky and attract a few extras, but the trend is still readily apparent; if you're getting fewer leads, you're likely getting fewer clients, which means you might have trouble paying your bills next month. The sooner you're aware of this, the sooner you can correct course.

For entrepreneurs in any profession, the thought of tracking KPIs can sometimes feel overwhelming. That's perfectly understandable. If this is all new to you and you've never tracked KPIs before, keep it simple in the beginning. Start by picking three business questions you want answered, find a way to measure the answer that you can track and update without too much work on a regular basis, and then start measuring it weekly. The more you grow as a firm, the more comfortable you'll feel, and the more metrics you'll be able to track.

IDENTIFY YOUR IDEAL CLIENTS

We know a two-lawyer family law practice in Seattle with a unique approach to their clientele. The firm keeps two separate offices, one representing men and one representing women. Each office is carefully designed to make their ideal client comfortable. The men's office is decorated in leather and oak. When a client visits, they're offered whiskey and cigars. The woman's office, on the other hand is decorated differently. Whiskey is still an option, but so are cocktails and champagne.

There are obvious risks involved in this approach. First, it might come off as cynical and overly gendered to some of their potential clientele. By assuming that all women prefer champagne to whiskey and cigars, these lawyers could be isolating an entire segment of the market who would otherwise hire them. On the flip side, all the prospective clients who have been looking to hire a champagne-friendly lawyer just hit the jackpot. From their first visit, that client is hooked.

The point is that this firm has clearly identified their ideal clients and built a marketing system and client service experience dedicated to the distinct category of people they want to work with. If you are a potential client who fits the firm's ideal, this place will clearly feel like the right fit for you. But if you don't fit their model of an ideal client, it will be obvious to everyone from the start that this firm isn't for you.

A successful firm of the future, more than ever before, must know its ideal clients, what they want, and how to find them. Firms should be equally clear on who they *don't* serve so they can spend as little time as possible on prospects who belong with a different firm.

This clarity around ideal clients brings a number of strategic benefits:

- It makes it easier to know what services, pricing, and delivery models your firm should pursue.
- It focuses your marketing messages and channels.
- It increases the likelihood you can develop a known brand, reputation, and credibility for a specific audience.
- It makes it much easier to filter out potential *bad clients* who might otherwise waste your time, leave bad reviews, or refuse to pay their bills.

In identifying your ideal clients, the more specific you can be, the better. These Seattle lawyers don't just target all men and all women. They target specific kinds of men and women. For instance, their ideal female clients are the stay-at-home wives of wealthy financiers and well-to-do husbands. While it may be true that not all women prefer champagne, just like not all men prefer whiskey and cigars, the men and women these lawyers are targeting do, and these lawyers know it because they've carefully defined their ideal client.

Now, picture your ideal client and start figuring out what distinguishes them from your less-than-ideal clients:

- What are the biggest worries keeping them up at night?
- How does this legal issue fit into the broader goals and opportunities in their life?
- What's the single most valuable thing a lawyer could do for them right now?
- Do they have a job? If they do, what kind?
- What's their income bracket?
- What clubs or sports or community groups do they participate in?
- Do they own a growth-oriented tech start-up, or is their company a multigeneration family-owned manufacturing facility?
- Are they fitness fanatics regularly following the latest yoga influencers on social media?
- Do they have childcare, or will they need to bring their kids to your office?

These questions are just random examples. Focus on the relevant and salient details for your practice and your clients, but avoid questions that might unnecessarily limit your ideal client or build in problematic bias and blinders.

Here's what we mean. When many businesses build buyer personas, they give them a specific name, describe what area of town they live in, and even define their race or gender. Any of those details could matter, depending on your practice area, but if they don't, then there's no reason to define them, lest you accidentally exclude great potential clients who just don't look like that.

For example, if you picture them living in a section of town with a predominantly white population, you might inadvertently end up with only white clients. If race doesn't matter to your practice area, then you've accidentally taken all potential nonwhite clients out of consideration.

Wherever you can, then, build bias checks into your persona process. In the majority of cases and with very rare exceptions, factors like race, gender, disability, and age shouldn't be relevant. Instead of defining unnecessary traits, focus on your ideal client's needs instead.

Please don't wing this. Get out there and start talking to people. Get your information directly from the source. Learn what past clients were up to three months before hiring you. Ask them what issues factored into their decision-making process. The more you can learn before creating your persona, the better.

YOUR IDEAL CLIENT'S JOURNEY

Another component of building your new business strategy is to deliberately design your client experience around their "client journey." A client journey is their full lifecycle from beginning to end. It starts when they learn they have a (legal) problem; continues through identifying potential solutions, selecting a solution, and experiencing the process of having their issue resolve; and ends after their case is closed and they become a referral for new clients.

Too many lawyers design their client experience to begin when a potential client is selecting a lawyer. But your potential ideal clients have more options than that for solving their problem.

Sure, there's your firm, but there's also a similar firm down the street, as well as a slew of other competing lawyers throughout town, plus DIY and lawyer-alternative options. Most clients put a lot of consideration into deciding the best way to solve their legal issue. Thinking in terms of the stages of their full journey allows you to understand what goes into that decision, and how you can deliver a great experience to your ideal clients throughout every stage of their journey.

For each stage of a buyer's journey, your job is to determine where your potential clients get their information, what they are looking for at that point, and how you can deliver them value and a great experience based on what they need at that time.

With each stage of the journey, it's important to be clear

on the potential client's goals. We tend to think that every message needs to be geared around making a sale, but that's not always the case. In fact, early in the journey, your goal is simply to attract attention and gain trust.

If you search for this topic, you'll find a variety of ways to approach it, but we'll frame it as a six-stage journey: *awareness*, *evaluation*, *conversion*, *onboarding*, *service*, and *loyalty*.

STAGE #1: AWARENESS

The moment a client becomes aware of their problem is the beginning of a potentially extraordinary customer experience. Clients in the awareness stage may not even think of their problem as a legal one quite yet. For instance, there can be many different reasons a person might ultimately seek out a family law attorney. One person might suspect their spouse is cheating on them, while another might simply feel like the spark in their relationship is gone. In either case, the client will likely pursue other avenues before deciding to seek out a lawyer.

No matter your practice area, try to understand and map out the earliest parts of your ideal client's journey. What are they thinking about? What are they struggling with? What questions are they asking? Where are they going for information or support at this phase?

Again, family law is an easy example. Generally, before people seek a divorce, they try to patch things up. If you back up three months or three years prior to the moment your client picked up the phone to call you, you'd probably identify some common behavior patterns—perhaps they sought out temporary living arrangements to take a break from their spouse, or perhaps they sought out a marriage counselor.

At this stage in their journey, it's definitely premature to start trying to sell them on a divorce lawyer because early on, most people will turn to other avenues for help way before they turn to a lawyer. Those other avenues can be many and varied—a Google search, a request for help from a friend, a curious glance through the phone book, or venting to Facebook. By finding ways to offer content, resources, or value to people early in the life cycle of their problem, you can create wins for yourself long before your future client even starts looking for a lawyer.

The awareness stage is all about building *trust*.

STAGE #2: EVALUATION

Once a potential client becomes aware of their legal problem, they'll start thinking about how to solve it, so they begin looking deeper for more information. Chances are they're trying to decide what type of solution to go with, thinking about the process and alternatives. While they might be thinking about lawyers, they're probably considering lawyer-alternative options alternatives as well.

This is your opportunity to leverage your brand and reputation (and any trust you built in the awareness stage) to position your firm as the right solution for them.

The more information you can provide during the early stages of the process, the more you can build trust and further your relationship with them. As they start to pick between different potential solutions, any relationship you've already built or value you provided early on, will make it much more likely you'll be the solution they turn to.

The evaluation stage is all about *positioning* yourself as the right solution for them.

STAGE #3: CONVERSION

Finally, a client is at the decision stage. By this point, they're very aware of their problem, and they're selecting between their options. They're ready to choose an option to go with. Maybe they're choosing between you and another lawyer. Maybe you've guided them through their journey so well that it's no longer a choice.

The conversion stage is when your marketing turns into

sales. As we'll discuss later in chapter 9, there are a variety of sales skills and tactics to make sure your ideal clients pick you as their solution.

STAGE #4: ONBOARDING

Once a potential client has become a retained client, a great experience should also include a deliberate welcome and onboarding process as the newest client of your firm. This is a chance to reassure them that they made the right decision in engaging you and to familiarize them with what it's like to work with your firm and what they can expect will happen throughout the engagement. What would it look like to delight and surprise every single new client that decides to hire your firm?

STAGE #5: SERVICE

When a new client is now onboarded, it's finally time to start delivering great legal services to help solve their problem. This is your opportunity to both be a great lawyer and represent them zealously but also to keep them engaged and supported throughout the life of their case.

STAGE #6: LOYALTY

When your ideal client's initial engagement is done, your

relationship should not be over. Whether your practice area included ongoing client work opportunities or this former client will now just be a source of ratings, testimonials, or referrals, make sure your full life-cycle experience has them feeling a sense of loyalty to you, your firm, and the work you could do for others in their situation.

CONDUCT COMPETITIVE AND MARKET STRATEGY ANALYSES

Most businesses develop a competitive analysis and market strategy early in their business-planning process. Lawyers running traditional professional services firms have usually not approached their market or their strategy this way.

It's easy to understand why they don't. As long as lawyers can practice law, they assume there's a market for what they want to do. They simply do what they know how to do. Traditionally, this has worked out for them.

While most firms might be able to list some of their potential clients and competitors off the top of their heads, chances are they haven't done much work to document this information. They often aren't asking potential clients how they first heard about the firm. They're not trying to find out what other solutions that client considered before hiring their firm.

This is a huge missed opportunity. Here's your chance to turn the guesswork into an essential foundational strategy.

WHAT IS COMPETITIVE ANALYSIS?

A competitive analysis forces you to define who your competitors are. Most lawyers only think they're competing against other lawyers but might not recognize that their clients considered an alternative solution to their problem before coming to them.

Make sure that your list of competitors includes the direct competitors of firms that practice in your practice area, in your jurisdiction, and serving your potential client base. Additionally, list the other ways your potential clients might solve their problems since you're competing against those solution providers too.

Once you identify your competitors, you begin an analysis to understand the strengths and weaknesses of how they're addressing the needs of your market. You can attempt to understand the details of what services they offer, their rates, what marketing messages they're sending to potential clients, and how they do intake and service delivery. The more research you do, the more you can learn about your competitors' targeting and messaging.

That said, you could do an infinite amount of competitive research or even hire a consultant to draft a thick report for you. Don't do that. The point of this exercise isn't to have exhaustive analysis or a report to gather dust. The point is for you and your team to document and agree on where else your clients get their problems solved and how you compare to those other solutions.

WHAT IS MARKET STRATEGY?

Once you've done the hard work and research into your competition, you can sit back and figure out what to do with that information in terms of market strategy. Trust us, you'll have a lot to think about—and you might even have fun doing it.

In your market analysis, your goal is to start looking for the gaps in who and how your competition is serving their clientele. Ask:

- Is my competition targeting the exact same people as I am?
- If yes, who's being left out?
- Is there a market I'm uniquely qualified to serve?
- Are my competitors serving their clients in ways the clients like?
- Are there ways to serve them better?

It's far easier to set up a practice targeted at an under-served market than trying to compete with everyone else in a crowded space. Most attorneys understand this and build their practices around a niche, but far too many fail to take this step, potentially missing out on huge opportunities.

A market strategy doesn't mean that you have to find a market that isn't currently being served. It just means you need to offer your services in a way that differentiates your firm. The more unique your services, the more you can dominate and win that market. For instance, one pair of lawyers we know have figured out how to do estate planning in a very comfortable way—so much so that their office feels like a living room. Because they were creative in how they benchmarked their business, they were able to stand out from their competition.

To conduct a robust competitive analysis and market strategy, we recommend the following approaches.

LEARN FROM YOUR CLIENTS

One of the most valuable ways to learn about your competition is to ask your current, former, and potential clients about their journey. Find out what kinds of options they considered before hiring you. If they still haven't hired you, or if they didn't end up hiring you, learn what other options they considered. Definitely talk with those who hired your competitors; it's a great way to learn about the kinds of experiences other lawyers offer.

Think outside of the lawyer space too. Most prospective clients avoid lawyers for as long as possible before it becomes inevitable that they need to hire one. How were your clients trying to solve their problem before they started looking for a lawyer? How can you remove that pain point and make them more comfortable working with a lawyer like you earlier in the process?

LEARN FROM YOUR COMPETITORS

There's nothing wrong with wanting to know what your competitors are doing. Start by searching the search terms you think your clients will enter into Google to see what pops up. Visit their website and any social channels they might maintain so you can get a sense of how they market to their clients.

There's no need to do this secretly or in private. In fact, often you can even speak directly with your competitors to learn how they position themselves in the market. Some of your competitors may be fairly open and friendly with you.

PRACTICE RELENTLESS INCREMENTALISM

You now understand some key areas of your business where it is essential to design and implement a strategy. From here, your job is to practice what we call *relentless incrementalism*—the process of slowly and relentlessly taking small actions that will bring you closer and closer to your ideal.

- **Set your goals.** While this was the focus of the previous chapter, it's the foundation of any good business strategy. Document your expectations, share them with everybody, and be mindful of how they may change over time.
- **Stay curious about how your market is changing.** Maybe your revenue is decreasing because the market has shifted somehow. If you're doing competitive analysis, you'll work out how the market is shifting.
- **Track your competition.** Watch where the market is moving and incorporate that into your strategy and goals. Say you're the only criminal defense law firm in Tallahassee without a podcast. You might not even realize it, but not having a podcast could greatly impact your business and client acquisition.

Now that you understand the basics, here are a few last things to keep in mind to keep your strategy on track.

BE CONCISE

What's your elevator pitch? How do you communicate what you do and why you do it to others? A good way to figure out your vision is to think about how many words you use when telling someone what you do. The more words you use, the more confusing your vision and values probably are.

GROWTH ISN'T LINEAR

Just because you've put some strategy behind your firm and operationalized your processes, that doesn't mean everything will run seamlessly from here on out. Things could go great for a week, a month, or even a year. No matter how well-run your firm is, however, certain challenges will find you eventually.

And that's okay. You might take a few steps forward and a couple of steps back. That doesn't mean your strategy isn't working. It just means one change cannot solve all your problems. Keep at it.

NO DISTRACTIONS

Sam's uncle is a successful dentist in Sioux Falls, South Dakota. Sam's uncle regularly had solicitations to invest in various side real estate or business deals. The deals may have been lucrative, but Sam's uncle would refuse them because he knew he could make more money focusing on what he was good at: being a dentist.

One of the keys to being successful is focusing on what you're good at and ignoring other distractions.

Unfortunately, many firm owners have trouble with this. They decide to pursue a different path for their firm on a whim or in their own self-interest, not considering the cost to their business and the low probability of success. Or like many entrepreneurs, they have "shiny object syndrome" and spend more time brainstorming new ideas and following new distractions than clearly focusing on their core.

While sometimes you may find it necessary for your business to pivot, when you aren't intentional about that process and don't clearly define a new direction for your firm, you risk losing more than you might gain. Having a sound strategy can keep you from pursuing costly whims and help you operate distraction-free.

DROP THE SCARCITY MINDSET

No matter your practice area, you *will* have competition, and you *will* struggle to find clients on occasion. What you make of that information, however, is up to you. Do you view the availability of clients, money, and billable hours as a scarcity, or do you view them as freely available to anyone with a sound approach for acquiring them?

Many of us opt for the former, and operating under a scarcity mindset is problematic for a number of reasons. Firstly, dollars, clients, and hours aren't as scarce as they feel. When you act like they are, you get off your game, and you start to make decisions that keep you small. Terrified that you'll be put out of business, you start trying to appeal to as broad of an audience as possible. Your elevator pitch gets longer. You start nickel-and-diming your firm's marketing budget. You start taking on cases that have nothing to do with your practice area. Running your firm from a position of scarcity almost always becomes something of a self-fulfilling prophecy in which you lose sight of the big, important things you could be doing to have big, important effects on your growth.

When you're strategic, scarcity doesn't exist. Instead of getting really big and trying to be everything to everyone, the way forward is to be really "small" and to find a clearly defined market you can do extra-valuable work for. Don't just be a personal injury lawyer, for instance. Be a personal injury lawyer who specializes in bike injury cases in major metropolitan areas. Define yourself by what you are *and* what you're not.

Your customers will appreciate you for it because you're

helping them find what they're looking for. When you go small and embrace a specific market, you offer confidence and peace of mind.

GET OUTSIDE SUPPORT

Great leaders know there is value in always learning, staying up to date on the latest trends and advancements, and collaborating with other industry leaders.

Whether through a coach, a mentor, a peer mastermind group, or an online community, small-firm leaders need support from outside their firm. This support can take many forms, including offering objective third-party feedback on hard decisions, providing emotional support when you're struggling, offering accountability and praise on your path to success, and learning ideas and best practices from the experience of people who have been through similar things before. For all of these reasons, a sustainable firm owner of the future must have regular structured interaction with professionals outside the firm.

When businesses can help each other, learn from each other, and engage with one another, it can be the case that everyone benefits.

GET A QUICK WIN

Craft your vivid vision. In Cameron Herold's book *Double Double*, he outlines a simple but profound exercise called "the vivid vision." Cameron's general framework is easy to do. Using the following questions, write down specifically what you want your firm to look like three years from now:

- If your firm had perfectly accomplished everything you would want in the next three years, how would it look?

- Who would be on your team? What would their roles be?

- Who would be your clients? How many would you have? What kinds of work would you be doing for them?

- What would your office look like?

- How would you feel day-to-day?

- What would your workday look like?

- How much money would you be making?

- What would your personal finances or possessions look like?

- Where would you go on vacation?

Answer these questions, or any others that feel relevant to you, with as much detail as you can to paint a clear narrative of what you and your firm could be in the next three years. Having this vivid vision can help clarify your why and help you think through specific steps that might be needed to actually achieve this vision.

Stephanie's father was a car dealer. While car dealers are typically known for being as competitive as lawyers, Stephanie's father actively engaged with and learned from other car dealers in his peer group.

Every quarter, he'd sit down with a group of car dealers that were about the same size and in a similar market as him. They shared everything, including financials. Everyone knew where everyone else ranked. For two days, they'd discuss *how* they did business, and together they would brainstorm how to solve problems facing their industry. Discussions like this made all of them better.

In essence, this is one of the things we do at Lawyerist. We often hear from people at our Lawyerist LabCon conference that it is the first law conference they have attended where their fellow attendees aren't competitive with each other. At LabCon, everyone feels proud to help each other, share information, and take steps to help others improve. When everyone lets their guard down, it creates an amazing environment to support learning and improvement.

If you're a leader, it's equally valuable for you to be challenged and supported by other leaders. Many of us at Lawyerist both facilitate mastermind groups and participate in them because we recognize how important they are for us. However you approach it, whether through coaching, mentoring, mastermind groups, or an informal peer network, we encourage you to surround yourself with other leaders who can help incorporate future trends into your strategy.

FIND A COACH OR MENTOR

What do all of the world's top professional athletes have in common? They all have a coach. Even those individuals who are clearly the best in their field. Why? Because they know that a coach sees a different perspective, can offer technical help, keeps them focused, challenges them, and inspires, motivates, and encourages them.

These same principles apply to you and your business. A coach will help you achieve bigger goals faster. Stephanie has been coaching lawyers for years (and has someone coaching her at the time of this writing) and has seen firsthand the tremendous benefits of coaching.

Sometimes, the coach is there to confirm your analysis and give you permission to take the next step.

Stephanie saw this when a Labster came to her knowing the lawyer needed to fire a member of her firm but was nervous to pull the trigger. Stephanie listened and confirmed her decision. Together, they created a plan for next steps, including a plan to address potential roadblocks that might creep up. They even role-played the upcoming firing conversation with the team member so the lawyer could be mentally ready. Finally, Stephanie held her accountable and checked in right after the scheduled firing date to hear how it went (and to make sure it actually happened). The Labster confirmed what a great decision it was and how she wished she had made it sooner (or knew how to hire better in the first place).

Other times, a coach can help you sift through the clutter of ideas in your head to see where to focus your energy and attention. Another Labster loves chasing shiny objects. He confessed that he once spent six hours researching the best telephone headset to buy for his firm. He now works with Stephanie every ninety days to create a prioritized plan for the quarter, supplemented by weekly check-ins to keep him focused. Now, occasionally when he's lost or stuck, he reaches out to clarify the next step and to get back on track.

So find a coach or group of people who can help you, challenge you, and push you toward creating a better firm. We know this isn't easy. But it's even harder when you're just doing it by yourself.

LET STRATEGY GUIDE YOUR CHOICES

Without a clear-cut strategy in place, you risk resorting

to the industry default strategy: find more clients, raise your rates, and bill more hours.

When you have a clear strategy, you are able to make every decision with intention rather than on the fly. You have a *why* for every choice you make (and every choice you *don't* make). For instance, not only will you know *why* you might want to add a new practice area, you'll know what it takes to get there and whether you have the necessary infrastructure and training in place. When you're grounded by a clear vision and values, decision-making is easy.

This is good news for you because, as you'll see in the following chapters, you'll have no shortage of decisions to make for your firm.

MORE RESOURCES

We've put together a set of free tools, templates, and worksheets designed to help you with your business strategy. You can download them at lawyerist.com/roadmap/resources.

CHAPTER 8

CLIENT-CENTERED SERVICES

Most lawyers would proudly tell you that their entire firm is focused around the client. While in one sense this is true—lawyers do represent their clients and take care of their legal needs—that's not what we mean by client-centered services.

When setting up your business, it's easy to think only of your own needs and goals. We're so focused on ways to make *our* jobs easier that we forget what it's like to be a client.

In this chapter, we're talking about the practical implications of what it looks like to start reframing the traditional lawyer-centered profession and begin creating client-centered services at your firm. These include:

- Rethinking your rates, fees, and how you structure your service prices.
- Deliberately thinking about client diversity, access, and inclusion.
- Crafting your firm's communication, intake, and onboarding around a great client experience.
- Tracking and learning from client feedback to improve their satisfaction.

Plan to create a client experience that shows that you care about them, that you understand who they are and what they need, and that you are the right person to take care of them from start to finish.

CLIENT-CENTERED PRICING AND FEES

A professor from Harvard Law School once told us a story from one of his students who started working as a small-firm associate after law school. The associate happened to have a background in software coding, and after realizing that one of the tasks he was asked to do was very repetitive, he decided to write a short piece of code to automate that repetitive task. In so doing, the student saved himself a considerable amount of time and freed himself up to work on more interesting projects, but because his time was billed hourly at his new firm, his innovative problem-solving cost his firm thousands of dollars in billable hours.

The partner he worked for was horrified. "Why would you do that?" he asked. "Now it takes less time; that's terrible!"

When you think about money as time, efficiencies seem like losses. There's nothing client-centered about that.

THE (SLOW) DEATH OF THE BILLABLE HOUR

If you ask your clients what they're buying, chances are they won't respond with, "I want to buy your time." And of course, they don't—they want to buy a solution, not units of time. And yet, this is exactly what hourly billing is. Most lawyers charge for their time, which often rewards them for being slow and inefficient, even if they don't mean to be. And when you're not motivated around efficiency, you have no incentive to come up with more cost-effective solutions to your client's problems.

By this point in the book, we hope you've already accepted the mindset that we actually *want* to provide clients with solutions to their problems in the most efficient and effective ways.

The truth is, while the death of the billable hour is still greatly exaggerated, in many cases, it's neither the most efficient way to price your services, nor the most helpful to your clients.

The small firm of the future has an expansive toolbox when it comes to pricing questions. Instead of hanging their shingle on the billable hour alone, they understand that they have a variety of options to price their services, from flat-fees and subscription services to unbundled services to value-based billing or contingency work and to, yes (maybe), even hourly pricing. While there's no one-size-fits-all approach, there is one core consideration: Are your rates designed around the goals and needs of your clients and structured in a way to align your incentives with your client's goals?

STRUCTURE YOUR PRICING AROUND VALUE

When you're focused on hourly billing, you're focused just on the time it takes to do your work. The way we see it, your pricing shouldn't be focused on time but focused on *value to the client* instead.

A lot of lawyers are apprehensive about this, but when you price your services based on value rather than time, you *and* your clients often come out on top.

When Hourly Billing Leaves Money on the Table

For example, since Stephanie hung up her lawyer hat and joined the Lawyerist team, she has had to hire two lawyers. The first came when she and her husband needed to secure an alcohol license from the Department of Revenue for their family's beer-distribution business. At the time, their application had stalled, and they couldn't move their business forward until it was approved. Stephanie felt happy to pay around $2,500 to get this problem solved.

The lawyer they selected not only had a good reputation but also a good relationship with the investigator at the Department of Revenue. After they hired him, the lawyer didn't speak much to them about pricing or value. Instead, he just defaulted to billing them by the hour.

A lawyer herself, Stephanie knew the dangers of hourly billing, and it freaked her out. Every time she talked to him, she tried to get off the phone as quickly as possible, painfully aware that the clock was ticking. She even offered to draft her own affidavit to reduce his workload.

In the end, Stephanie's apprehension turned out to be unwarranted. In fact, she ended up getting the better end of the deal. The lawyer was able to get their application processed with just two phone calls—which hardly took any time at all. A few weeks later, Stephanie and her husband were pleasantly surprised to receive a bill of just $748.

In this instance, because the lawyer chose to bill by the

hour instead of on value, he left money on the table. Stephanie hadn't hired him for his ability to send out briefs; she hired him because he had a valuable connection for getting their application approved, a connection that she was willing to pay $2,500 for.

Notice anything else about that story? Stephanie may have known her lawyer was charging her an hourly rate, but she had no idea what her final bill was going to be. In that case, she came out on the better end of the deal, but for the duration of the representation, she was worried it would come out the other way.

When Hourly Billing Surprises and Angers a Client

The second time Stephanie had to hire a lawyer, however, she wasn't as lucky. That time, she expected to pay about $5,000 for the legal services she would receive. But because of some unexpected issues that popped up during the deal, she ended up with a surprise bill for $9,450.

Most lawyers probably don't set out to make their clients feel outraged and betrayed. But after receiving that bill, that's exactly how Stephanie felt.

What's more, this entire situation could've been avoided with a simple, open, and honest conversation up front and along the way. All Stephanie's lawyer had to do was tell her how the new issues were going to significantly increase the amount of time they spent on the deal. This would have empowered her to make a decision about how much she was willing to spend and what her budget allowed. Instead, she was at the mercy of the lawyer and stuck with a bill that was nearly twice what she had budgeted. A client *always* finds it more helpful if the lawyer defines the work they're going to do and is given the power to make decisions that impact their case and the bill along the way.

ALTERNATIVE FEE MODELS

Hourly billing isn't always bad. Sometimes time *is* a good measure of value. The problem is that most firms treat time as the only measure of value, and that's definitely not true. Adding some alternative fee models to your tool kit will help you do a better job pricing your services according to value.

Flat-Fee Pricing

The best fee structure of all, *when it works*, is a flat fee. Flat fees give you and your client certainty. They allow you to think outside the hourly billing box and reward you for finding more efficient ways to get your client the result they want. And of course, you don't have to deal with the tediousness of tracking your time or trust accounting (in most jurisdictions; as always, consult your local rules).

Flat fees are pretty simple: you charge X for Y. There are at least three important challenges in doing flat fees well:

1. Figuring out what to charge (X).
2. Describing the scope of work (Y).
3. Anticipating surprises.

Figuring Out What to Charge

When you are starting out with flat fees, the easiest way to figure out what to charge is to look back over similar matters and come up with an average, plus a small safety buffer. In the short term at least, it's a good idea to continue tracking your time to make sure your estimates work out.

But it's also important to get out of the hourly billing mindset and start thinking about how you could deliver better value in fewer hours. Refine your workflows for efficiency. Consider what you can automate or outsource. Stop doing things that aren't required and don't add value. Come up with alternative strategies that save time but get you to the same result. Use your freedom from hourly billing to get creative!

Describing the Scope of Work

Take the time to clearly describe what is included in your fee—and what isn't. This is a good way to head off any surprises as well. For example, if you are quoting a fee for a litigation matter on the assumption it will not go to trial, exclude trial from the scope of work. If the case does end up going to trial, you can quote another fee. You can probably even put a price tag on it up front, so that your client can take that cost into consideration at the outset.

Make sure you actually discuss the scope of work with your client. You want to be certain you are on the same page so they don't feel like they are a victim of the "small print" in your retainer agreement if something outside the scope of work comes up later on.

Anticipating Surprises

In addition to describing the scope of work and discussing it with your client, talk about surprises. In every representation, there are surprises with the potential to make your estimate look silly. If you are billing by the hour, you'd just keep billing (although hopefully you would give your client a heads-up first). If you are using a flat fee, surprises mean coming up with a "change order" for the extra work after you communicate the surprise to your client and discuss how it will affect the outcome.

Communication is key when it comes to flat fees. The whole point is to make sure you and your client know what you are going to do and what it will cost.

Unbundled Services

Unbundling means limiting the scope of work to a specific task or project. Not everyone needs full, traditional legal representation. Some clients are happy to handle some or most aspects of their matter themselves with help from a lawyer for specific tasks or on an as-needed basis. For example, you might ghostwrite a complaint or summary judgment memorandum for a client who is handling a lawsuit on their own. Or you might review an estate plan your client downloaded from a website and customized themselves.

It's not always appropriate, ethical, or legal to unbundle services. But often it's just fine, and unbundling can help your client feel like they are in control of their legal matter and its cost.

Unbundling can work out great for you too. In many cases, your effective hourly rate will be higher for unbundled services, even though your client is paying you less than a full-representation client would pay. Done well, unbundling is a win-win for you and your client.

Sliding-Scale Fees

Some law firms use a sliding scale to adjust the fee according to the client's ability to pay. The most common approach is to assess the client's income and compare it to the federal poverty guidelines. For example, you might offer 50 percent off your hourly rate to anyone at or below 150 percent of the federal poverty guidelines, 40 percent off to anyone at 151–200 percent, and so on. You get to decide what the scale is for your firm, of course.

You can use a sliding-scale fee for any kind of billing arrangement, including flat, hourly, unbundled, etc. Just be careful to define the scope of work and estimate the base fee before you determine your client's eligibility for a discount. It defeats the purpose of a sliding scale if you offset them by subconsciously setting higher flat fees.

Subscription Pricing

Some kinds of legal matters lend themselves to a subscription model, where your client automatically pays a set amount per month. (You can use other billing periods, of course, but monthly usually makes the most sense.) For example, you might have a real estate client ask you to handle all their closings, which average out to ten per month. It should be pretty easy to come up with a fair monthly fee. Or you might have a small business client interested in retaining you as its "outside in-house counsel" (or "outhouse counsel" as Sam likes to say) so it can seek your advice on an as-needed basis. In that case, you might charge a monthly fee for unlimited phone calls, emails, etc., and quote additional fees for additional work.

The important thing with subscription pricing is to make sure you deliver the value of the fee every month. You don't want to spend a lot of time and effort reassessing the fee every month. Nor do you want your client to be constantly wondering if the subscription is worthwhile. Focus on tying the recurring fee to the recurring work, defining the scope of work, and making sure your client will be open to discussing additional fees for additional work.

DIVERSITY, ACCESS, AND INCLUSION

Who do you serve? Who are your main clients? What are you doing to accommodate them? Is there anyone you're excluding in the process?

Earlier in this book, we discussed society's access to justice gap. Sadly, the lack of access to legal services and legal solutions falls hardest on people without resources, people of color, people with disabilities, and others who have historically been marginalized.

As we also mentioned earlier in the book, the demographics of our society are rapidly changing. Separate from access to justice concerns, more and more of the core paying clients of law firms don't look like they did twenty or fifty years ago.

And all of this is a good thing, for two reasons.

First, we hope you agree that improving access to lawyers for the traditionally underrepresented is a good unto itself. It is an increase in the fairness of justice and the rule of law and all those other ideals we hope you still support.

Second, even if social justice isn't a passion of yours, finding more and better opportunities for our legal services to be inclusive to clients who don't look like us also dramatically increases our pool of potential clients. So it's also good for business.

In a wonderful podcast conversation we had with Haben Girma in Lawyerist Podcast #147—the first deaf-blind graduate of Harvard Law School—she notes that almost sixty million Americans have some sort of disability. When you consider the potential mobility or hearing limitations that often come with aging, the population of people with disabilities grows every day.

As advocates for justice but also as savvy business owners,

we have a huge opportunity to better design our firms to be inclusive and accommodating of a more diverse future client base.

Many lawyers have never considered whether their services, their office space, or even their website are accessible. Many resources are available to help you design your firm to meet modern accessibility standards so that people of all abilities can access your firm—which, objectively speaking, will improve the firm for everybody. The problem is, most of us aren't aware of such services, nor do we take the time to inform ourselves.

Think carefully about the population you are serving. What's life like for them? How can you make their experience better in every way? Ask yourself:

- What's it like for a blind person to interact with your site?
- Would a gay or trans person see themselves represented within the context of your firm?
- Would a person of color feel welcome in your office?
- Would a person of a lower socioeconomic status be able to get to your office? A client from a poorer background might not be able to physically come to your office because that requires taking time off work, getting on three buses, and paying for childcare.

When firms give their attention to issues like this, they're able to come up with creative solutions to solve them. For instance, we know of an estate planning firm in Minnesota that markets itself as a mobile law office. They have a small fleet of vans that they drive around to meet clients in their homes. This is an innovative way to think about client-centered services and accessibility.

And that's the key: to *think* differently about diversity, accessibility, and inclusion. During a discussion of accessibility in one of our podcasts, our guest Heather Hackman (#105) made an excellent case for why we should stop thinking about people with disabilities as "others"—that is, as people somehow different from us. The fact of the matter is that all our bodies are constantly changing. Just because we can do something now, that doesn't mean we'll be able to do the same thing five years from now. At some point, most of us will need at least some special accommodations.

When viewed from this light, it's not just about serving people born with a disability. It's about adapting to the changes we might all experience. For example, our eyesight deteriorates as we get older. If your client base is an older population, you might use a bigger font on your website or the signage on your door.

There's a lot more we could say about this conversation,

but here's the bottom line: Whatever your perspective, you need to build a system that allows people to engage with you in a way that makes them feel comfortable and included.

CLIENT COMMUNICATION

In Clio's 2018 Legal Trends Report, the tech company asked lawyers and clients about their expectations for receiving communications and information.[11] The broad strokes are fairly unsurprising; some information is best delivered face-to-face, while some information is better delivered on the phone, in an email, or via a web portal. As long as the method of communication matched clients' expectations and preferences, the clients were happy.

When delivering client-centered communication, meeting their expectations and keeping them happy should take priority. So what's the best way to do that?

GIVE CLIENTS A CHOICE

To be a client-centered business, you need to put yourself in your client's shoes. When you do this, think about how your client would prefer to communicate with you. Consider what they actually *need*, not what's easiest for you.

---

11   Clio. "2018 Legal Trends Report." 2018. https://www.clio.com/resources/legal-trends/2018-report/

The first step is to talk to your clients about communication. As their lawyer, be prepared to communicate in any way they prefer, as long as that method is adequately secure. Perhaps that's through email, perhaps that's through a web portal, or perhaps that's over the phone or via a video chat. Whatever the case, it's your job to find out.

However your client prefers to communicate, educate them on some basic privacy considerations. For instance, if your client prefers email, it's your job to explain why they shouldn't use their work computer to send and receive email.

That said, also take the nature of your message into account. Your client may prefer email, for instance, but email is a terrible way to deliver bad news. Sometimes, communicating through multiple channels can be helpful. For instance, there's nothing wrong with delivering a complicated concept via email, but it's probably a good idea to follow up with a phone call to make sure your client understands everything.

HOW OFTEN SHOULD YOU COMMUNICATE?

Many clients report that they don't know what to expect when it comes to communication from their lawyers. When they haven't heard back on their case in a while, many start to panic.

We'll leave it to you and your clients to determine the exact cadence of your communications. Some clients will appreciate regular check-ins, while others will assume that no news is good news. Whatever the case, have a conversation about this early on during the onboarding process so you can jointly set appropriate expectations.

Also, as a general default, overcommunicating is probably better than not communicating enough. Once you establish a relationship with individual clients, you can learn more about how they prefer to communicate. More often, you'll find it less disruptive to dial the communication back than to dial it up.

CONSIDER THE EMOTIONAL CONTENT

Your goal is to do what the client wants. Often, this is more nuanced than it seems. In fact, a large part of building a client-centered relationship is learning how to get at what your clients are *really* after, not just what they tell you. Depending on your practice area, the emotional stakes could be pretty high.

Practice empathy. Try to make the unsaid said. Believe what they say, but consider the possibility that there's more to the story, whether for the good or for the bad.

DROP THE LEGALESE

Lawyers love to send off those epic five-page cover-your-ass letters, which are usually dripping in legalese.

Don't.

They're a waste of time for everybody. Your clients won't read them, and you're probably spending too much time drafting them. Whatever is written in five pages of legalese can usually be written as bullet points on a single page. They're easier to draft and easier to understand; everyone wins.

When you start leaning into the legalese again, just ask yourself: Are you communicating in a way that your clients will understand and find useful?

Whenever you can be concise, be concise—and you can be concise anywhere. Shorten your retainer. Format it so it's not only easy to read, but easy to look at, even if that means hiring a professional to redesign your document template. If you're intending to bind your client to an agreement, they should know what they're signing.

TEST OUT VISUALS

Most lawyers think in text. We use words as our primary form of communication, but a lot of people don't operate this way. Think about whether there are opportunities to communicate with your clients through diagrams or illustrations. (Don't be patronizing about this. We aren't trying to make the law childish; we're trying to find ways to communicate ideas to our clients in the best ways for them to hear us.)

One time at a training, Stephanie took part in an unusual exercise. Stephanie and the other participants were split into two groups. One group was given a complex concept that was explained in text, while the other group was given the same concept, explained visually in an illustration.

After the two groups reviewed the content, they were asked how well they understood the concept being conveyed. Perhaps unsurprisingly, the group who was given the illustration demonstrated a better understanding of the concept.

There's nothing that says all your communications have to be text-based. Graphic illustrations can work as well, and so can videos. Whatever the case, look for ways to communicate with clients that resonate best with them.

FEEDBACK AND SATISFACTION

When it comes to a client seeking feedback and satisfaction, we have two big recommendations:

1. Don't skip this step.
2. Keep it simple.

A lot has been written about advanced methodologies for collecting customer or client feedback, but if you're not using the data in an actionable way, then all you're accomplishing is annoying your customers.

Naturally, a system that annoys its clients is counterproductive. Nobody wants to receive five automated emails a day asking them to rate a product or service, and yet this happens all the time. The whole point of feedback and satisfaction surveys is for you to grow and improve as a firm, not to create an annoying, noisy experience for your clients.

The method or tool you decide to use to gather feedback doesn't matter as much as the questions you want answered. Whether you're going old-school or taking a tech-enabled approach (where there's no shortage of software solutions), there are three basic questions you want answered:

- How did you hear about us?
- Would you recommend us?
- Is there anything we could do better?

Once you have your answers, it's on you to turn your

feedback into categorized data. It's no use keeping that information in your head or on a piece of paper in your client's file. At a minimum, put that information into a spreadsheet and use it for benchmarking, goal-setting, and learning.

Certain feedback tools will also give you the opportunity to deepen—or perhaps salvage—your relationship with your client. For instance, if someone gives you a low rating, your platform could automatically file a support ticket for you to follow up on. Alternatively, if someone gives you a glowing review, your platform could redirect your client to another platform like Google or Yelp so that they can share their praise publicly.

As long as these tools aren't annoying your clients, you can create a virtuous cycle with your marketing. When you serve your clients well, not only will you get valuable marketing data but also potential referrals.

If your clients give generic, one-word responses, don't be afraid to dig deeper. You want to get to the truth, not to inflate your ego. Perfect experiences rarely exist in any context in the business world. With that said, don't inflate your own system either. If you're pushing your clients to give you high scores in order to meet some self-imposed quality standard, you're doing it wrong.

If you're using benchmarks to compare your current performance with past performance, or perhaps event to project future performance, that's great. You need context to provide better client-centered services, but if you're just using benchmarks as incentive for performance bonuses, you're likely not learning anything valuable from the process.

Don't be afraid to check in with your clients more than once. While you don't want to be annoying, we recommend seeking feedback throughout your working relationship—once shortly after you begin representation, and then periodically both throughout and after you close a case. If representation goes on for a year and a half, for instance, ask for feedback at least two to three times.

Make engagement as effortless and satisfying for the client as possible. The more focused you are on creating a client-centered service, the better position your business will be in the long run.

SEIZE YOUR OPPORTUNITY TO STAND OUT

All law firms are in the customer service business. Asking how you can serve your clients in a helpful, sustainable, powerful, and additive way should always be at the forefront of your mind.

One of the best ways to do that is to provide a deliberately designed client experience. If you can do that consistently, then your clients will gladly help spread your message for you. As you consider the tactics we discussed in this chapter, ask yourself what you can do to go the extra mile. How do you wow your clients right out of the gate? What can you do that's unexpected and that sets your firm apart from all the other firms out there?

We'll leave the specifics up to you. Just make sure that whatever tactics you choose align with both your values and your brand, and that they aren't gimmicky. Even something as simple as a friendly phone call the day after your client signs their retainer can go a long way in creating a lasting impression.

> **MORE RESOURCES**
>
> We've put together a set of free tools, templates, and worksheets designed to help you craft client-centered services. You can download them at lawyerist.com/roadmap/resources.

CHAPTER 9

CLIENT ACQUISITION

For a lot of small-firm lawyers, when the going is good, they don't worry about marketing at all. They get busy doing client work, stop spending money on ads, and stop going to business networking events. Then, when those cases close, they suddenly realize they had no pipeline feeding next month's cases, and they scramble to jump-start all of their old marketing activities with the hope of getting busy again for a while. Naturally, this isn't a sustainable strategy for predictable success—and yet so many lawyers find themselves endlessly trapped in this cycle.

How can lawyers be so good at practicing law and so bad at consistently having the pool of clients they need to achieve their goals?

The simple explanation is that most lawyers weren't

taught much about client acquisition—in other words, marketing and sales. Most of us came out of law school believing that landing clients and growing a firm was as simple as "networking" over coffee, lunch, or drinks. For some lawyers this was more or less true way back in the twentieth century, but outside of a few well-established lawyers coasting toward retirement, that's certainly not the case anymore.

Simply put, if you're not perpetually marketing your firm, developing your brand and reputation, and improving your client-onboarding and sales-conversion processes, your practice is at risk.

Some lawyers understand this, but even that group often struggles to see results. They're quick to embrace marketing as an important concept, but they fail to start from a clear strategy or to implement and improve it regularly.

Some of their efforts work, and some of them don't— but they never *really* know which was which. When their efforts inevitably stall out and business slows back down, they find themselves back at square one, frustrated at spending so much energy to see such mediocre results.

For other lawyers, words like *marketing* and *sales* are still dirty words that sully their professional dignity. They insist that their firm is built entirely on *relationships*. To an extent, this might actually be true for them, but it isn't really much of a sustainable growth strategy for the future for you.

So let's get one thing clear right out of the gate. *Marketing* and *sales* aren't dirty words. To improve your client acquisition and make better use of your time, you need to know at least the basic concepts and approaches that drive modern marketing and sales practices. That's what we're going to give you in this chapter, helping you find your potential ideal clients and converting them into happy, paying success stories.

START WITH THE BASICS

A good marketing strategy eliminates guesswork and instead prioritizes specific data-driven experiments of a variety of tactics each tested under a clear hypothesis. Because you're intentional in your approach and because you're testing and tracking your results, you can learn from both successes and failures and improve your efforts in an iterative fashion. To understand how this process works, let's start with the basics.

THE DIFFERENCE BETWEEN MARKETING AND SALES

It's not worth belaboring the point, but so we can all be

on the same page, it's worth making some distinctions between the related (and often overlapping) concepts of sales and marketing, both of which should work together as part of your full *client acquisition* strategy.

For our purposes, your firm's *marketing* function is the work you do to get potential ideal clients to see you as the best solution to their problem and to contact you about helping them. This includes:

- The work you do to establish your brand, reputation, and authority.
- Your efforts to get prospective clients to know about you and how your firm might help solve their problem.
- Your tactics and systems for getting potential clients to contact your firm.

Not all marketing activities are meant to result in a sale. Establishing trust as an expert in your area is an important part of a client acquisition system but, on its own, isn't directly about finding clients.

Sales includes any conversation where the goal is to convert a person into a paying client. Here is where your marketing efforts pay off and where you bring all that information to bear to convince someone that you're the right person for the job.

Marketing and sales are part of a continuous process. Success in one contributes to success in the other, but they serve different needs for your business.

THE INBOUND MARKETING FUNNEL

Depending on what modern business book you pick up, the marketing and sales process is often represented as a funnel, a flywheel, a life cycle, a canvas, or some other useful visual indicator.

None of these models are right or wrong, and you're welcome to follow whichever resonates the most with you. But we think the "inbound marketing funnel" is a valuable starting point for engaging your ideal clients along their journey.

The funnel is meant to capture the *awareness*, *evaluation*, and *conversion* phases of your ideal client journey (discussed in chapter 7).

In this view of client acquisition, you begin with a broad pool of awareness-stage potential clients based on your ideal client persona. These are your *potential leads*—people with whom you want to establish trust to eventually make a connection and build a relationship.

Your awareness-stage marketing activities involve creating great content that is valuable to your potential clients.

From that broad pool of potential leads, try to move them through your funnel to create real leads by engaging them as they move into their evaluation stage.

Most people don't call your law firm the first time you engage with them. In fact, it usually takes several touchpoints to convert someone into an actual lead. A touchpoint can be a variety of activities—a web ad, a podcast interview, a tweet, a blog post, a newspaper article about you, and so on. With each touchpoint, you want to provide value and encourage them to take action to reach out to you.

For this evaluation stage, you need a great website as the hub of your online reputation and the source of most of your inquiries (even word-of-mouth referrals are going to Google you and find your website before calling), you need a variety of sources of traffic to that website, and you need clear "calls to action" on your website, making it easy for interested potential clients to contact you.

When they contact you, you'll want a deliberately designed reception and intake process to make sure that people contacting your firm receive a great initial experience and get a call or consultation scheduled.

Eventually, a certain number of leads have moved all the way down the funnel and have scheduled time with you. At this stage, you'll use your sales and conversion skills to encourage them to sign your retainer agreement.

As we've already discussed, though, the journey doesn't end at this point. Now that you have a newly signed ideal client, you'll still need to do the post-purchase work of onboarding, service delivery, and earning loyalty.

While some of this might seem theoretical, you'll want to actually map out your funnel and attach data to it. We'll provide you with a free spreadsheet template you can download at the end of this chapter to keep track of all of this.

HOW TO BUILD A SUCCESSFUL CLIENT ACQUISITION PROGRAM

Now that we've covered the basic framework—marketing versus sales and the inbound funnel framework—let's get into building out your client acquisition system. In the following sections, we'll discuss these cornerstones of a healthy sales and marketing program:

- Establishing your brand, authority, and reputation
- Outlining your marketing plan
- Designing a modern website

- Offline and online tactics to create "traffic"
- Converting leads into clients
- Data-driven learning from metrics and tracking

BRANDING, REPUTATION, AND AUTHORITY

Many people assume a law firm's brand is its logo.

While a logo can be one aspect of your brand, it's only a tiny component of a much more important concept.

There are dozens of competing and confusing definitions of the word *brand*, but in general, the concept is that your firm's brand is the overlap of your reputation and perception in the market with the promise and perception you're *trying* to create in the market.

We don't want you to get bogged down in the differences between branding, reputation, perception, or promise. The point is that your client-acquisition system starts with your work in aligning your *actual* reputation in your community with the reputation you *want* to have and establishing yourself as a trusted authority to your potential ideal clients.

Through this concept of branding, whether it was consciously created or not, your firm already has a brand. The question is whether your brand represents what you want it to or not.

Be Authentic

Imagine you're trying to brand yourself as a hip lawyer who helps young people manage their estate plans, but when a client walks into your office, they see you're seventy-five (not that there's anything wrong with that) and wearing a rumpled suit. Your office is a scattered mess of documents, and you can't even log onto your computer (despite having had the same computer for years).

Do you see the disconnect?

Don't pretend to be something you're not. Be authentic. Build a brand that authentically reflects both you and your firm's values.

Be Consistent

Then make sure all your branding efforts are aligned. For example, the way you answer a client's phone call during intake should be well aligned with the way you designed your website and marketing brochure. When someone thinks about your brand, you want that picture in their head to be as clear and consistent as possible.

Become an Authority

For most people, when they have a problem, they want to

hire the *best*. But most clients aren't looking for the best *overall* lawyer; they want the best lawyer for *them* and their *specific* needs.

There are a number of reasons to establish yourself as an authority in your area of law for your ideal-client market.

First, signals of your credibility and expertise—and any early value you can provide—are the surest ways to establish *trust* early in a potential client relationship. The more a potential client (or referral source) sees you as someone likely to offer a great solution, the more likely you are to attract that lead.

Second, developing actual expertise—not just being *seen* as an expert—makes it much more likely you'll know how to successfully solve your client's problems and have happy clients after their representation.

Finally, a business built around reputation, authority, and expertise is much more likely to create a strong unified brand that will allow it to succeed in the face of competitors and outside change.

So how do you *become* an authority? Through hard and smart work.

The answer will vary somewhat for different practice

areas and client types, but developing expertise today doesn't look very different from developing expertise a generation ago:

- **Learn** all you can about your clients' legal needs, the laws that apply to them, and the strategies that work for solving those problems.
- **Practice** solving those problems with your clients to gain experience understanding how these solutions actually work.
- **Deconstruct** the things you've learned or experienced to see if there's a new or better way—your firm's way—of solving these problems repeatedly.
- **Teach** others as a way of sharing your expertise and also as a tool to force you to clearly structure what you've learned. This teaching can take the form of blogging on your site, publishing a podcast, writing bar journal articles, presenting CLEs, teaching a community education class, or lecturing at your law school.
- **Lead** others in your client industry or the legal profession through service on volunteer committees, policy advocacy work, or mentoring others in your practice area.
- **Solicit** recognition from others about the great results you've delivered for clients and referral sources through industry awards, client ratings, or peer referrals.

HOW ~~LAWYERIST~~ SAM DID IT: BRAND, REPUTATION, AND AUTHORITY

We'll give the same advice we gave when discussing buyer personas: ask your clients why they decided to contact or hire you. If they were impressed by how you presented yourself, you've obviously done a good job. If they hired you despite poor branding, then you'll want to reconsider how you're presenting yourself.

Sam, for instance, consciously branded his firm around the look and feel of a punk rock poster—all black and white with red accents. He knew his consumer rights clients were the kind of people who felt let down by big corporations, so he decided a punk ethos not only represented who he was as a person but also communicated that he was a lawyer who would stick it to the man.

It worked. Whenever Sam asked his clients why they hired him, many of them said it was because Sam looked like somebody who would stick it to the man. With such close alignment between the image Sam wanted to portray and the image his clients were receiving, Sam had built a strong brand.

Later in his law career, Sam shifted his practice to represent tech startups, which meant he needed to rebrand away from the punk ethos and toward a more startup-centric identity. First, he moved his office to get closer to his ideal clients and to create a space that would make people want to do business with him. He also considered his clothing choices, deciding that he would rarely, if ever, wear suits when meeting with clients. It wasn't just because Sam hated suits (which he did), but he also knew that it would create a better dynamic with his clients that broke the "stuffy lawyer" mold.

- **Promote** your expertise by noting it on your website and in your writing—not as an act of narcissistic ego-boosting but centered around your clients and how your experience and authority are the right solutions for their problems.

Brand Identity

While your brand is not your logo, your logo is a part of your brand. In fact, your *brand identity* is the collection of things like your name, logo, design and document standards that present your firm in a consistent way to evoke the kind of engagement you want your brand to convey.

Your brand identity should carry through every aspect of the client experience, from marketing and sales to onboarding and referrals. Your brand identity and brand standards should be documented, followed consistently across the work of your firm, and include some of the following:

- Firm name
- Logo
- Color scheme
- Fonts and typography
- Work product document formatting standards and template design
- Look and feel of marketing materials

- Stationery and business card design
- The tone, voice, and style standards of writing at your firm
- The images on your website

Every brand chooses what to check off the list. Your brand might decide to not have business cards and only have a digital presence, for example. As long as you're making a conscious choice, that's great. As with composing music, sometimes it's not about the notes you play, but the notes you choose not to play.

DATA-DRIVEN MARKETING PLAN

To create your marketing plan, you'll need to understand a number of the concepts we discussed earlier, such as who your ideal client is and what their journey looks like. Using that information, your marketing plan can be quite straightforward to include seven sections:

1. **Goals:** Your SMART goals for client acquisition.
2. **Ideal Client:** A description of your ideal client, including information on who your ideal client *isn't* so everyone in your firm can know to avoid bad clients.
3. **Brand:** A description of the reputation and authority you want your firm to have with your ideal clients.
4. **Ideal Client Journey:** Outline the stages of your ideal client's journey, including their needs and goals at

each stage and what people, organizations, or marketing channels currently get their attention at each stage.

5. **Competitive Analysis:** Describe the other solutions your ideal client considers and how you compare to those competitors' strengths and weaknesses.

6. **Tactics and Experiments:** Make a prioritized list of tactics to experiment with for each stage of the ideal client journey, including when you'll test each, and how you'll measure success so you can know whether it's working or not.

7. **Data and KPIs:** Make a list of the data you will need to track on a regular basis to test your tactics experiments and see if you're on pace to achieve your SMART goals.

WHICH TACTICS SHOULD YOU USE?

First, be clear on your goals, your budget, and what you expect to get out of your effort—in other words, your return on investment (ROI). Then start looking at different marketing tools and tactics that might work to serve those goals. Depending on your brand, your practice area, and even your location, you will find that different tools, tactics, and strategies work for you better than others. Determining which ones work for you will involve a little bit of trial and error:

- Pick a tactic.
- Learn how to deploy it.
- Test it, spending as much time and money as necessary to see some results.
- Evaluate those results. What worked? Could your approach be improved in any way?
- Based on your results, determine whether that tactic is worth pursuing further.

We encourage you to be as methodical as possible. What you don't want to do is pick a marketing tactic on a whim and then waste all your time and money trying to make it work. Take Twitter, for example. Many lawyers hear Twitter is a good marketing tool. So they join. Then, without bothering to learn any best practices or taking the time to listen to their clients there, they send the same message out every day: "Have you been injured in an accident? Call me today!" Nothing about that approach makes sense.

Create a marketing strategy with a specific purpose and plan for implementation that fits with what your ideal client wants. Consider which platforms you might use at different stages in the journey. Then be objective. Look at the data to help you determine the success of your efforts.

WHERE ARE YOUR CLIENTS?

Part of understanding your ideal client is understanding where they spend their time and, maybe more importantly, where they spend their *attention*. If none of your clients are on Facebook, for example, then it makes no sense for you to market on Facebook. Figure out where your clients' attention is and experiment with that first.

You don't have to be everywhere all at once. You just have to be where the majority of your ideal clients are. While it's tempting to just set up shop on Facebook or Twitter, sometimes a billboard can prove more effective. Or teaching CLEs. Or teaching community ed classes. Or stapling your business card on the bulletin boards of hipster coffee shops. Or maybe even Snapchat. Figure out where your people are and find a way to be seen there— assuming you can *be seen* there authentically.

WHAT'S YOUR MESSAGE?

Criminal defense lawyers love to brand themselves as the toughest people on the planet. But does that actually resonate with clients? Maybe—although we suspect that what most clients want is someone who will answer the phone and be there for them during what is likely the darkest and most embarrassing moment of their life.

Whether you're a criminal defense lawyer, a real estate

lawyer, or a family law lawyer, the story you tell is the lifeblood of your brand. Take some time to consider your story and what about you will resonate most with your ideal client. Perhaps your story is built on name and reputation, as is often the case with criminal defense lawyers, or perhaps it's built on empathy and compassion—putting your *clients'* story before your own.

WHAT'S WORKING FOR YOU?

Think about your marketing strategy as an adventure to find where your customers are and how they prefer to interact. When you do this successfully, your strategy immediately becomes clearer.

Once you find something that works, stick with it—and then double, triple, and quadruple down on it. Conversely, anything that only has marginal value should go.

A certain amount of experimentation is valuable too, but don't go overboard. To create a balanced approach, use the 80/20 rule, where 80 percent of your strategy is dedicated to proven techniques, and 20 percent is dedicated to experimentation.

Following this rule keeps you from tumbling down too many rabbit holes. It's tempting to want to try every new tool and technique we hear about, but it can also be counterproductive—especially if you spend too much time testing out a dead end. Test a tool well enough to know if it works or not. If it doesn't, bail. If it does, throw it into the mix and keep going with it.

Another reason the 80/20 rule is so great is that it can come in handy when you need a backup plan. Imagine, for instance, that you get 90 percent of your business from Facebook, but suddenly, the Facebook algorithm changes, and you don't get any more business. In case of such a disaster, it's worth having other tactics ready to make up for it.

MODERN WEBSITE

In the twenty-first century, if your business doesn't have a website, then you are doing it wrong.

And not just a website. Think broadly about your digital presence—social media pages, Yelp and Google reviews, and so on.

Your website is the most important piece of your digital mix because (1) you have the most control over it, and (2) it's likely your most visible online asset (especially on Google). In some sense, at least in the business world, if Google doesn't know about you, then you don't exist.

Even if you're more the old-school type and you generate

most of your leads through networking and lunches, you still want a website. It's the easiest way to validate referrals. Imagine this: after a networking lunch, one of the people you met gives your name to a prospective client. What's the next thing that client does? They pull out their phone and Google your name. If your website doesn't pop up, that's going to send a red flag.

Aside from being an important way to validate referrals and confirm that you exist, your firm website can serve many other purposes:

- If you have a blog, it can serve as the hub of your inbound marketing, where you provide teaching and value to prospective clients.
- It is likely the primary destination for traffic and a source of leads for your firm.
- It's a place to engage prospective and existing clients.
- It's your primary place for establishing your authority and managing your reputation.
- It can be a source for recruiting and building your team.
- With the right website tools, it can be a place to deliver client services through communication portals, account management, or online billing.

Before you set out to design your website, know what your goals are.

Separately, but just as important, create a site that is fast, easy to use, personalized, clear, and mobile-friendly.

The good news is that you don't need to break the bank creating an effective website. But plan for it to be an investment and be willing to spend the market rate. In the long run, the firms who try to cut corners either pay more in site fixes and lost revenue or waste a bunch of their valuable time trying to do too much themselves.

Invest an appropriate amount in your website and work with your designer to create an attractive, well-branded site that maximizes the client experience (seriously, please build your site around your clients, not your ego). Then be prepared to populate your site with useful content. Without it, your site is nothing more than a digital business card and is unlikely to persuade a visitor that you are the person who can finally help solve their problems.

If you need to find a designer, we can help. We've created a law firm website designer review and recommendation page on Lawyerist to help you find the right designer for your goals, budget, and time frame. You can visit it at lawyerist.com/reviews/website-designers-seo/.

GET A QUICK WIN: TEN ESSENTIALS OF A MODERN WEBSITE

Over the last decade, we've advised thousands of lawyers on getting professional, client-friendly websites, and we've recognized great website design in our annual Best Law Firm Websites contest, available at lawyerist.com/marketing/websites/contest/.

In that time, we discovered a few common traits we think all law firm websites need:

1. Start with a well-defined goal.

2. Highlight your call to action.

3. Focus on your client-centered value proposition.

4. Welcome mobile devices with responsive design.

5. Avoid visual clutter.

6. Use bold colors and striking images.

7. Take advantage of typography.

8. Design for accessibility.

9. Optimize for search engines.

10. Secure your website.

For more information on these ten tips, check out lawyerist.com/marketing/websites/.

BUILDING OFFLINE AND ONLINE TRAFFIC FOR LEADS

Once you have a great website to serve as the hub of your inbound marketing funnel, it's time to identify tactics for generating potential-ideal-client traffic to your site.

To be clear, we aren't at all concerned with how much overall traffic (or "hits") your website gets; counting generic visits is a vanity metric.

What we care about is finding a variety of ways to bring as many potential ideal clients to your site as possible—visitors who aren't a fit for your firm shouldn't matter to you.

If you Google "How to get traffic to your website," you're likely to find a number of online tricks for increasing generic visits to your site. That's not our concern here. What we want to do is outline sustainable online and *offline* tactics—activities that are aligned with your brand and designed for your ideal client journey—to get more quality leads contacting your firm. Thankfully, many of the activities that will most successfully drive high-value traffic to your website are also the same signals Google looks for when ranking your site *and* are the same activities you use to build your reputation and authority.

SOURCES OF ONLINE TRAFFIC

When thinking through data-driven experiments on which digital marketing activities to pursue for your firm, we suggest you consider a mix of the following:

- Social media engagement with potential ideal clients, referral sources, and the media.
- Blogging on your firm website—or a separate legal blog.
- Guest posting on other legal blogs.
- Paid social media ads (and "boosting") to promote content that demonstrates engagement with your audience.
- Participating in online forums, communities, and groups.
- Hosting a podcast or appearing as a guest on other podcasts.
- Hosting webinars or teaching on other webinars.
- Starting an email newsletter.
- Offering a valuable free download to potential clients as an incentive to join your email newsletter.
- Sharing your blog posts or podcasts with others in the industry to occasionally earn a mention (and a link) from them.

SOURCES OF OFFLINE TRAFFIC

As we mentioned earlier, even word-of-mouth referrals will likely Google you and visit your website before contacting you. Because of this, you can even think of your offline advertising, networking, and reputation-building activities as being traffic sources to your website, including:

- Speaking and teaching.
- Writing in magazines, books, and newspapers.
- Networking at happy hours, events, or through your hobbies.
- Event sponsorships and conference attendance.
- Volunteering and bar association leadership.
- Brochures (and even your business card).
- Traditional advertising like print ads, TV, radio, billboards, or the yellow pages.
- Earning awards or other recognitions.
- Being a quoted source to the media or being featured in media coverage.

YOUR CALL-TO-ACTION AND LEAD INTAKE SYSTEM

Whatever the source of your traffic, once people see your ad or visit your website, make sure to ask them to contact you. The annual winners of our Best Law Firm Websites contests all feature a prominent phone number, an email contact form, or calendar scheduling link at the top of their homepage. This is your call to action, and it should be deliberate and prominent on your site, but it should also be designed for your clients. The goal isn't to shock your clients with a big red CALL US NOW! button but to engage them where they are so they want to contact you.

When they do email or call your firm, make sure you've deliberately designed your intake process.

Have a pleasant person answer your phones in a consistent way using a script you've designed (and improved over time) to serve three purposes:

- Welcome them and make a connection.
- Assess whether your firm can help them and whether they fit your potential ideal client profile.
- Reassure them that your firm is the right answer to their problems and convince them to schedule a consultation.

Make sure you provide potential clients with a great experience starting the moment they contact you. Your intake calls must reflect the tone, image, empathy, and value you want the rest of your client experience to consistently convey.

A great intake system is a cornerstone in translating all of the work you've done in marketing, branding, reputation, and website calls to action into booked appointments.

CONVERTING LEADS INTO CLIENTS

So now that they've made their appointment, it's time to have the sales talk.

But first, let's get the obligatory disclaimer out of the way: *Be sure that you're following your jurisdiction's rules about how to ask for business and offer services to a client.*

No matter how your ideal client journey or inbound funnel progresses, there comes a point—the conversion stage—when you will have to ask your prospective client for business. The sales conversion process is crucial, yet many lawyers we know don't put much thought into designing it and delivering it consistently.

In those firms, every new lead is handled on a whim. One prospective client is called back a day after their consultation, while another is called back three days after. Some aren't called back at all. Some prospective clients might hear a pitch about why working with a particular firm is better, while others don't.

From the moment your prospective client has entered the conversion phase—whether it is via a phone call, meeting for a consultation, or submitting an online form—follow a carefully thought-out process that leads to that ideal client to sign an engagement letter. Be intentional when designing this process, decide exactly what you want to say, and document everything.

If you did your job during the awareness and evaluation phases, your prospective client already knows who you are and how you can help them. You may still have some educating to do, but the focus is no longer on the broad strokes of their legal need or whether you're a trusted authority on their issue but rather on how your firm will work with them to solve that problem. In the end, sales happen when you ask your ideal client to hire you.

Take advantage of this opportunity. Educate your clients on exactly how you will guide them through the legal process. As a lawyer, it's your job to help clients understand what to expect in terms of what the process will look like, how long it'll take, and what their role will be. Then ask. Most importantly, be clear what happens when expectations aren't met. A client should understand how and when the lawyer has a right to file a motion to withdraw.

After all that, it's time to talk money.

ADDRESSING COST OPTIONS

When Sam was in law school, he worked in the boating department of a local, independent outdoor sporting goods store. The price range of boating equipment varied considerably. For instance, a customer could spend anywhere from $50 to $1,000 on a kayak paddle.

A big part of Sam's job was to explain the differences between the low-end paddles and the high-end paddles so his customers could understand what compromises they'd be making by choosing the cheaper option. After walking them through the options, he would then make a recommendation based on what the customer's stated needs were and what level of experience they had kayaking.

Your prospective clients have a similar consideration when choosing between a service like LegalZoom (the $50 paddle) or a small-firm lawyer like you (the $1,000 paddle). Your job is to explain what someone would get by using a software-created document and what they would get instead by working with you. Be honest, and don't be afraid to acknowledge that your client *does* have other options.

After talking it out with your prospective client, you may determine that they're better off with the $50 paddle instead. If that's the case, tell them so. Don't pressure someone into buying from you when you're not their best option.

If they probably should go with the $1,000 paddle but

they choose the $50 paddle instead, feel free to tell them why you think it's a bad idea, but don't overstate your case. Respect that your potential clients have a choice when hiring you and that the decision is ultimately theirs. Besides, even if they go for the $50 paddle now, they may decide that they'd be better off with the $1,000 paddle down the road.

GET COMFORTABLE TALKING ABOUT MONEY

Every client should understand what your services will cost or how they'll be priced before they engage you. Unfortunately, many lawyers are uncomfortable having the money conversation. Don't be.

First, don't be ashamed of making money. As long as you're selling your services at a fair price that delivers value to your clients, then you don't owe an apology to anyone for asking what it's worth.

Second, by managing client expectations about pricing, payment policies, and what's expected, you build trust and clarity into the lawyer-client relationship.

There are different ways to approach this, depending on how you charge for your services. When Sam worked on contingency, for instance, he understood how important it was for his clients to understand what that meant and how everybody would get paid once it was all said and done. To make the process easier, he came up with a Venn diagram that laid it all out.

If you bill by the hour, you may find prospective clients balking at your $350-an-hour rate. Part of this is perception; many clients assume that lawyers bill in the same way a person does at an hourly job: you clock in every morning, and then clock out every night. Naturally that's not the case, but it's your responsibility to explain to your client that you only bill for the actual time you put into the case. If you get up and go to the bathroom, for instance, that clock turns off.

Whatever the case, when it comes time to name your price, give the number and shut up.

We mean it. A good salesperson doesn't only know when to talk, but when *not* to talk as well. Sure, there might be an awkward pause after you name your price, but you're under no obligation to fill it. We've seen plenty of lawyers talk themselves out of a fair rate with little provocation. They'll start at a $1,000 fee, then immediately knock that rate down to $750—then down to $600, then to $500—

simply because they couldn't handle the awkward pause. Don't be scared of that pause.[12]

After giving your prospective client the chance to respond, you may need to discuss their concerns or objections, you may need to discuss payment terms, or you may need to clarify how your service is worth that amount, but let them show you the path to finalizing the agreement.

DATA AND TRACKING

How much does it cost you to acquire a client?

Which is your most effective marketing tactic?

How much does it cost, all in, for you to deliver a particular service?

Most lawyers can't answer questions like this, which is one of the reasons why lawyers often don't see the value of a marketing plan.

The result is a bit of a mixed bag, with lawyers making many of their marketing decisions based on gut instinct

---

12   Emma Brudner. "7 Reasons Awkward Silences...Are Actually Powerful Sales Tactics." Hubspot. August 9, 2017. https://blog.hubspot.com/sales/reasons-awkward-silences-powerful-sales-tactics

and hunches. We understand this impulse, but no decision should be made in a vacuum.

Once you make it part of your process to collect data across all your marketing channels, you'll see that you gain a tremendous amount of insight for a minimal amount of effort. For instance, you may discover that, while one tactic might be significantly more expensive, it also results in five times as many ideal clients walking through your door—which makes it your most effective activity overall.

Alternatively, you may realize that a tactic that you thought was valuable is more or less a bust. For instance, you may take pride in the fact that you meet with upward of seventy-five prospective clients a month in free consultations, but if only two of those seventy-five people are signing with your firm, is it really worth your time? Maybe. You may just have a sales problem. After seeing these dismal numbers, you may decide to add follow-up calls to your meeting process, which could lead to a significant spike in conversions.

A simple fix like this could lead to a significant boost in revenue, but if you're not collecting data and tracking your marketing efforts, you'll never have the insight to make these crucial adjustments.

THE WINNING FORMULA: CLIENT ACQUISITION COST

The basic formula for determining your client acquisition cost (CAC) for each distinct marketing activity you use isn't all that difficult:

> (Out-of-pocket expenses + time-value invested in the activity) / number of signed clients = client acquisition cost

Let's walk through this equation step by step, and then we'll give some examples.

First is cost—both in money and time. The financial side should be easy; if you paid for a Google ad, for instance, you know exactly how much you spent. Determining the cost of your time (or your employees' time) is pretty straightforward as well; however, most lawyers fail to take time into account.

For example, they may think of in-person networking as free, but when they start adding up the time cost—not to mention expenses at the event itself—they'll realize it's not free at all.

To determine your time cost, you just need to track how much time was spent on the activity multiplied by the value of your time (whether or not you bill by the hour).

THE VALUE OF YOUR TIME

If you bill by the hour, it's easy to set a value on your time. Value your time for all activities in the firm—client work, marketing, office management—the same and calculate all of your activities according to your average billable rate.

This will align your incentives so that time spent on one activity is considered of equal cost to any other activity, and activities that aren't worth your "value" are done by someone less expensive than you.

If you could charge a client $250 per hour right now, but instead you're working on tweaks to your website, make sure that those website tweaks are worth *at least* $250 per hour to your firm and that no one else on your team could make those same tweaks for less time or cash.

If you don't have a set hourly rate, calculating your time value is a little more complex but should still be straightforward. Without making it too complicated, a simple approach is to take your base salary (more on that in chapter 13) and multiply by three (as a rough proxy for capturing the firm overhead and profit margin that should be built in to *every* employee's base salary).

APPLYING THE FORMULA TO COMPARE TACTICS

Let's apply the formula to your marketing activities. Say you're using two different marketing tactics, paid Google ads and attending networking events, and you want to know which method is more effective.

Last month, you paid $750 for Google ads, and $250 in your time to create and manage the ads. During that time, you signed two new clients as a direct result of those ads. Put it all together, and you'd have something like this:

($750 + $250) / 2 clients = $500 per acquisition

There you have it. Paid search ads cost you $500 per client.

Now, what about your networking events? Last month, you paid $100 on these events—on cocktails, donations, etc. You also spent $750 in time. As a direct result of those events, you received three new clients through referrals. Putting it all together, you'd have something like this:

($100 + $750) / 3 clients = $283 per acquisition

You may have thought networking events were practically free, but in actuality, these events cost you $283 per new client.

Still, you can't help but notice that cost is almost half as much as your online marketing efforts. These networking events may carry significant time cost, but they're also your most lucrative marketing channel. What could you do to capitalize on that information? Double down. In this scenario, you could find a way to give more presentations at more local community groups. Get yourself out there. But remember to keep tracking these numbers over time to see if your cost per client goes up or down or if another marketing channel becomes a better use of your resources.

WHERE DO YOUR MOST VALUABLE CLIENTS COME FROM?

Once you've learned how to calculate the cost of acquiring a client, take it further. Figure out where your most valuable clients come from. This may seem like extra work, but when you're on a limited marketing budget, a little extra work here will help you get far more bang for your buck.

In fact, even if you only take on a few new files a month, these data are still valuable. Small firms often only need to track these numbers monthly or quarterly. While you'll have a clearer picture the more you measure, even tracking semi-frequently is better than not tracking at all.

To determine where your best clients come from, compare the average *lifetime value* (LTV; the estimated total amount you expect the client to ever spend at your firm) of clients acquired through different channels. For instance, the average lifetime value of a client acquired from your Google ad campaign might be $8,000, while the average lifetime value from your offline networking might be $3,000. When you add in these numbers and compare your two activities, suddenly the imbalance in acquisition cost seems less consequential.

In this case, your Google ads are generating $16.00 per dollar spent ($8,000 LTV / $500 CAC), whereas your networking is generating $10.60 per dollar spent ($3,000 LTV / $283 CAC). Adding in a lifetime value analysis flips your marketing strategy on its head.

We've seen the benefits of this approach in our own practices. For instance, when Marshall practiced at a medical malpractice firm, they turned away about 97 percent of cases that came through the door. On its face, that number might seem astronomical. How could they let so many cases slip away? Simple. The 3 percent of cases they did take had an incredibly high average lifetime value. Had their firm not been selective, they would have been wasting time on lower-value cases.

ONBOARDING, SERVICE DELIVERY, EARNING LOYALTY

Now that you've built a sustainable client acquisition system of high-performing marketing tactics and are winning at converting leads into clients, it's time to live up to your brand promise and begin the second half of your ideal client's journey.

The more you help your clients along the rest of their journey, the more likely they are to leave positive reviews, refer others in need of the same services, pay their bills on time, and otherwise sing your praises. The better you can maintain that relationship, the better your standing in the marketplace.

MORE RESOURCES

We've put together a set of free tools, templates, and worksheets designed to help you with client acquisition, marketing, and sales. You can download them at lawyerist.com/roadmap/resources.

CHAPTER 10

SYSTEMS AND PROCEDURES

Law firms can be complex and fast-moving organizations. In the face of this speed and complexity, the firm's leadership has the important role of building systems to deliver consistent, high-quality, and error-free legal work to clients. But for many firms, their systems and procedures live in their attorney's heads, or they're slightly reinvented as each case progresses and risk not delivering consistent experiences to each client.

The key to solving this, and getting great work done consistently, is to have documented systems and procedures that your team follows, a consistent way for managing projects in your firm, and systems in place for you and your team to follow good productivity and time-management techniques.

In our view, delivering legal services is nothing more or

less than project management. Viewed through that lens, then, delivering excellent legal services for your clients is about developing your skills in project management and systems.

These systems start with you. *You* set the tone for your firm. Get all those "common sense" ideas out of your head and onto the page. Give your employees and clients the peace of mind they (and you) deserve. That way, everything you want to happen *will* happen—in the way you want it to.

Besides, there's another benefit to creating consistent systems: it exposes the holes in your process. You may be a mad genius with plenty of great ideas on how to get things done, but you likely haven't considered every single scenario. Once all your ideas are out of your head, you'll be able to work with your team to make them even better.

In this chapter, we're going to teach you how to treat your systems and procedures with the importance they deserve. At least one person in your firm should be actively documenting everything you do to set yourself up for success in the long run.

STEP #1: PROCESSES

Imagine you've just hired someone new to your firm,

someone who you're trusting to help on an upcoming case. As the hearing date approaches, the unknowns start piling up in your head. Did you serve subpoenas? Are your exhibits labeled? Do you have all the copies you need? Did anyone order a court reporter? Nobody likes to feel this kind of panic—and if you document your process properly and in a way that anyone can follow, you won't have to.

Many lawyers, especially solo lawyers, never document how or why they do things. They just do them. It's easy to understand why. Documenting takes time, and the more time you spend here, the less time you're billing—and the less money you're making.

That may be true in the short term, but failing to document your systems and procedures will only create problems for you in the long run. The second someone on your team leaves, or the moment you decide to take on new staff, you'll see what we mean. Suddenly, you have to explain to someone what you do, but you have nothing to explain why that thing is important to give your clients an exceptional experience and nowhere to point them to in order to get them going in the right direction. And if you're a true solo, it's tempting to think, since there's no one else to train, that you don't need these things in writing. But getting it down on paper (or in a piece of software) is the surest way to make sure you're focused on delivering your services consistently and finding ways to improve what you do.

GETTING STARTED

At its core, a business is simply a series of systems that work together. When you pull back and think about your business, you'll see a few primary types of systems:

- **Client acquisition systems:** Use these to attract prospective clients and convert them into paying clients.
- **Workflow systems:** Use these to map out different business processes and project management best practices, such as client service, administrative duties, marketing, and so on.
- **Financial systems:** Use these to manage your firm's money.
- **People systems:** Your hiring, staffing, or management systems outline the ways you attract, hire, and manage your team.

Again, you and your team probably already have an idea of how you approach these systems. You've just never bothered to write that approach down.

Luckily, getting started is easy—and decidedly low-tech.

Start with a single document and name the most important core repeated categories of work in your firm. Then pick one, and outline the broad-overview basic steps you follow to do that work. You've just documented a process! Start setting aside small amounts of time on a regular basis to add details (eventually even checklists or screenshots or form templates) and to outline the other systems. But take them one small step at a time. You don't need to craft a three-hundred-page manual yet. You just need to start making relentless, incremental progress on capturing the way work is done in your firm.

To save yourself time down the road, begin documenting any new process as soon as you've done it more than once. This can be fairly informal at first; just open up a blank document, and start typing out a bullet-point list.

The next time you're drafting a particular type of document, make a bullet-point list. Start with the broad strokes of the process, and then fill in the details as you become more accustomed to it. Once you've had time to build this process out, formalize it and add it to the manual.

Over time, your procedures manual will get closer and closer to complete—although with ongoing improvements and refinements and new business experiments to document, it should always be a living document that is never fully done.

THE BENEFITS OF DOCUMENTATION

Documenting your systems and procedures has many benefits to your business. Here are some of the big ones.

Optimization

If you want to optimize your work, sit down and take time to capture how you move from start to finish. It's inevitable that you'll see ways to work faster and more efficiently. Going through the process of documenting and identifying what you're doing will force you to look for ways to optimize and produce a better work product.

We know one firm whose team does this weekly. They're constantly looking for ways to make their work faster and better—while improving the overall product and maintaining client satisfaction.

Your goal shouldn't be to go faster for the sake of it. That's not what optimization is all about. Instead, find ways to be more efficient with your time.

Learning

The process of writing a procedure helps you understand it better—and therefore makes you better at it. Often, you're writing the procedure for yourself, not for anybody else. Writing your process and teaching it is valuable for helping you refine it yourself.

Better Client Experience

Another benefit of documenting your processes is that it creates more opportunities for wins for your clients. Going through this process encourages you to think carefully about your client experience, which should always be at the center of what you do. By creating and then scrutinizing each of your processes, you inevitably find ways to create a better client experience that aligns with your mission.

Fewer Mistakes

There's no denying that legal work—not to mention running a business—is a big and complex job. When dealing with complex issues, our brains simply can't hold all the necessary information at any one time. In fact, the more information we try to keep in our heads, the more likely mistakes will be made. Either team members forget to communicate with each other, or they simply assume that someone else is handling the tasks that need to be done.

When you document your workflows and checklists, you allow your brain to let go of the small things. That way, you have more space to focus on the more important legal issues that only you can handle. As a result, you can work more confidently knowing everyone on your team understands their role and what's expected of them.

Easier Delegation and Training

When we document our processes, it becomes significantly easier for us to delegate work to other team members because they understand what they need to do. They aren't left in the dark about how to approach a problem or complete a task.

Many lawyers have a hard time letting go of work and delegating tasks to members of their team. They don't believe other team members will approach the work in the same way they do. This leads to lawyers feeling frustrated and holding on to work.

Your training will become more effective when you document your processes. Not only will you understand what your new hire needs to know, but you will better communicate how you expect the work to be done.

When you train according to properly documented processes, your team will know exactly how to take care of these kinds of tasks. Everyone will have the resources they need to do their job.

Feedback and Reviews

Often, supervising attorneys struggle to give meaningful feedback to their team members. Documenting your processes greatly improves this process. With proper documentation, you have an objective tool to determine whether someone is doing what's expected of them. As a result, you will be able to give more specific and less random feedback.

Scaling and Selling

If you ever want to scale your business, you have to document your systems and procedures. For example, opening a new office will be much harder without documented procedures.

Similarly, if you ever plan on selling your firm, you create much more value for your buyer when you enable them to hit the ground running. While they'll inevitably put their own stamp on your former business, having a blueprint on which to build is invaluable.

WHAT ARE THE BEST DOCUMENTATION TOOLS?

There's no one preferred tool for documenting systems and procedures. Generally, however, the most common tools fall into one of three categories:

- **Physical manuals:** Some firms will print and hand out an actual procedure manual. In a paperless office, this method can feel a little antiquated, but it gets the job done if necessary.
- **Shared files:** A shared file (or folder) that all members of your firm can find and work from (or maybe even suggest edits together) can be an easy way to create and share your procedures.
- **Wiki tools:** You can also create your procedures using private wiki tools. These are private, password-protected websites that offer collaborative, interconnected pages (just like Wikipedia, but private to your firm).

When selecting a tool, experiment and find one that works of you. Just make sure that it's central, easily accessible, and shared with your entire team.

HOW LAWYERIST DOES IT:
PROCEDURES MANUAL

Lawyerist goes by the following system to create and manage our company's procedures.

One person on our team is assigned the task of coordinating our procedures manual and keeping it up to date. That manual then lives as a group of separate documents, all in the same shared folder online, and all set up so that team members can collaboratively add feedback and make edits to them.

We have procedures documents for:

- Board of directors meetings

- Hiring procedures

- HR/employee manual

- Content marketing (articles, blogs, and social media)

- Ad sales and partnerships

- Community success

- Technology and data

- Finance

- Operations and office management

Each document is structured around the functions and regular tasks for that topic and includes a step-by-step process for how each function is done. The instructions are often supplemented with screenshots of someone doing the task or links to the place the task actually occurs.

For one hour every other Monday, our entire team blocks off their calendar so we can all work on improving the procedures manual. Sometimes that means making tweaks or suggesting small improvements to an existing process. Sometimes that means starting to outline the basic steps of a new process. Some of our procedures are highly optimized workflows with detailed instructions. But others are currently barebones. It's not that we have a perfect document. It's that we all dedicate a little regular time to making it incrementally better.

STEP #2: PROJECT MANAGEMENT AND WORKFLOWS

We think providing legal services is about effective project and workflow management and while processes are related to project management, the two are nevertheless distinct. Your processes help you understand the basic steps for getting something done, while project management and workflows help you complete those steps in a timely manner and within the context of your workday.

Advanced readers or those who dig deep into project management methodology may choose to eventually make different distinctions, but for the purposes of getting started, let's think of project management and workflows this way:

- **Project management** is the framework you'll use for one-time activities, like launching a new website, deciding whether to launch a new practice area, or managing a complex case that isn't like your others.

- **Workflows** are the framework you'll use for ongoing, repeatable work that follows a consistent outline every time, such as your intake process, your monthly invoicing process, or your standard cases or client engagements.

Modern project management is focused on relentless and iterative improvements. There are many good approaches to this, with names like *lean*, *agile*, *scrum*, and *Kanban*. While the specifics of each are different, they all follow a similar premise: whatever you're planning on building, your vision doesn't have to be fully realized before taking action. To get started, all you have to do is identify your core needs, identify who the client or in-house project customer is, determine the first steps that need to get started, build those out, and then find ways to improve your system.

Discussing these methodologies and their nuances and distinctions is beyond the scope of our book, but this project management framework can be used both for managing a complex, one-time case and for your firm's business projects. Regardless of which methodology fits best for you, they share many similar themes:

- **How much time do you spend defining your goals?**

It's so important to be clear on the front end about *what* you want to achieve. If the project is a case, what is the client's real goal? If it's a firm project, what is the client-centered goal for your firm? Throughout the course of the project, check back in with those goals. How have they changed? How are you keeping those goals at the forefront?

- **How are you collaborating with your client?** Are they involved and interested in your representation? Are the decisions you're making along the way aligned with what they've told you they want?

- **How are you communicating?** Are you communicating directly? Are you writing unnecessary five-page letters when a page of bullet points would suffice? Are you actively listening to their questions, input, and feedback?

- **Are you simplifying the process?** Are you moving cases through your pipeline efficiently and effectively? Are you looking for opportunities to make complex things as clear as you can?

- **Are you working to iterate and improve your process each time?** Are you learning and adapting as you go? Are you reflecting retrospectively?

Here, we encourage you to do a little research, pick a methodology that looks like it might work for you, and try it out. Eventually, you may want to tweak that process to suit your own needs, but before you do, it's important that you understand the two basic systems: projects and workflows.

PROJECTS

A project is a standalone complex activity that has a beginning and an end. For example, a complex case is a classic example of a project. A client walks through your door, signs a retainer, and begins their project. The project ends when you close the case, whether that means getting a judgment, finishing an appeal, signing a contract, or finalizing a divorce. Your endpoints will be specific to your practice area.

That said, you'll have other projects in your business as well, such as implementing your new project management methodology, training everyone to use the firm's project management software, and creating a new client welcome package. In any of these examples, there is a clear beginning, middle, and end.

To map out your project, create a series of columns in this order:

- To-dos
- In progress
- Completed

Under each one of these, you will then list out the tasks that need to be done, are being done, or are done. That first element, your to-dos, are crucial. What do you need to get done for a case—and when? Once you have clarity here, you can begin to establish the relevant deadlines.

That's the basics of project management. Eventually, you will want to create a board like this for each project your firm is currently working on. Tech can be invaluable here. There are plenty of project management tools out there that will help you customize, standardize, and automate the project management system that works for you. The trick is to commit to the project management process and make sure that every project in your firm follows your format.

WORKFLOWS

A workflow is different from a project in that it the framework of the ongoing or repeatable systems in your firm (again, cases or business activities). Examples might include:

- You have one major workflow for all standard client-related services. This could begin with marketing and end with closing the file.
- You have a workflow for marketing, which is ongoing on social platforms and elsewhere.

- You have a workflow for your intake process because you're constantly taking on new clients or trying to turn potential clients into actual clients.
- If you're a personal injury law firm, you have a workflow in which all of your cases move through discovery, presuit negotiations, or settlement discussions. After you send a demand letter, you try and engage in discussions, draft the complaint, and file it. Then you go through discovery, summary judgments, pretrial, trial, settlement, and then you close the file.

You probably won't have much trouble identifying the primary workflows in your firm. Most firms probably have a handful of major workflows that drive most functions in their firm, which might include:

- Your client intake process
- Your new client onboarding and welcome process
- Your billing and collections process
- Your case closing checklist
- Your blogging or social media posting process
- Your monthly bookkeeping and accounting activities

The tricky part is identifying the stages. As an example, let's imagine we're managing the workflow of a litigation project. Just like with your projects, start by drawing a series of columns. Each column represents a different stage of the litigation process. If you've properly identified your systems and procedures, you'll know exactly what these are. For the sake of our example, let's say the stages are as follows:

1. Draft the demand letter and negotiation
2. Draft the complaint
3. Enter into settlement discussions

As you move through the workflow, your client moves from column to column.

The distinction between projects (big one-time things) and workflows (repeating or ongoing things) might not always be obvious, and that's okay. As you engage in creating systems for managing both, you'll likely recognize opportunities to build repeating workflows from things you thought were more like one-time projects but that actually do recur.

Whether for project management or workflow management, once you get into this, one of two things will likely happen:

1. You'll fill the walls of your firm with columns of sticky notes.
2. You'll adopt some form of project management or workflow automation software.

In either case, build your system to accommodate both projects and workflows.

KEEP ITERATING AND IMPROVING

Now that you have a list of both the projects and workflows in your firm, it's important that you maintain quality and continue to iterate. To do that, first, always be clear on your goals for every project and workflow. Second, establish regular check-ins for each project and workflow. With each check-in, ask the following three questions:

1. **What is going well that you should keep doing?** This includes any experiments which you came up with to improve the process.
2. **What is going poorly that you should stop doing?** If any of your experiments didn't work, stop doing them. If you've implemented a strategy that isn't working for a case, drop it.
3. **What should you try going forward?** Think about how you can modify any tactics or strategies for the next case.

If you keep asking yourself those three questions, you'll be able to think of ways to improve the process and how you handle projects. The more you test strategies, the more you can evaluate and improve them over time.

These check-ins will prevent you from getting caught in the trap of doing things just because you've always been doing them. Engage honestly with the process so you can constantly identify opportunities to improve and get rid of the things that aren't working.

DISCIPLINE YOURSELF

Project management is a discipline, just like being a lawyer is. For many people, project managing is a full-time job.

You won't be a full-time project manager yourself, and you may not be able to hire one to help manage your firm either (although some firms we know have done exactly that). If you take the time to learn how to manage projects according to one of the methodologies we discussed earlier, then you will be well-equipped to apply these principles in your own firm.

STEP #3: PERSONAL PRODUCTIVITY

When you have six, twelve, or thirty different cases, you have to figure out what you need to work on day to day. This isn't easy—and in fact "time management" is consistently the biggest source of stress and pain revealed in most lawyer surveys.

Unfortunately, the project management methodologies

we just discussed won't always tell you what you need to be working on at any given time. Most of those methodologies were developed for people only working on a couple of projects at a time. Lawyers typically work on dozens of projects at a time, as well as on the workflows that make the firm work. Further, lawyers are frequently juggling a variety of different priorities and ongoing case, client, and team communications that can change those priorities, require attention, or become a distraction.

That's a lot to manage, and a lot of pressure. In the legal profession, you simply cannot afford to miss deadlines or fail to respond to emails or letters. When you miss deadlines, you start losing clients, money, your job, or even your license.

To stay on top of your deadlines while managing your business (and your inbox), you must have a personal productivity system. A project management system is also important, so you know what your deadlines and the big picture are, but a personal productivity system ensures that you know what to prioritize to work on *right now*. This is the trick to making sure that you're not constantly putting out fires.

There's no one system that works best. In fact, we encourage you and everyone at your firm to do some research to find the system that works best for them, even if different people in the same firm adopt different systems. The key is that each person should have one. Popular approaches include:

- Books like *Getting Things Done* by David Allen, *First Things First* by Stephen Covey, *Zen to Done* by Leo Babauta, or *Deep Work* by Cal Newport.
- Apps like OmniFocus, Tasks, Wunderlist, or Todoist.
- Print planner systems like the Bullet Journal, the Covey Planner, the Panda Planner, the Best Self Planner—or our own **Lawyerist Productivity Journal**! We designed our Lawyerist Productivity Journal to incorporate a number of principles from the systems described in this chapter but adapted specifically for small-firm lawyers. It's available at lawyeristjournal.com/.

GETTING THINGS DONE

Though we encourage you to dig into any of the systems we just mentioned, the one that resonates the most with us and was most influential in the design of our Lawyerist Productivity Journal is *Getting Things Done* (GTD). The philosophy behind Getting Things Done is to get all the unnecessary baggage out of your head, out of your inbox, or off your desk and into a single dedicated system where everything will be organized and nothing will be lost, and that you can return to whenever you want. This system is reliable; you won't lose anything.

When you know everything you need is there, you can check out for the evening or the weekend. You can be present with your family. When you come back to work, you can pick up your trusted system where you left off.

Here is the basic approach. First, whether you have paper, a full email inbox, or scattered sticky notes, set aside a small amount of dedicated time on a regular basis. Then work to the following steps:

1. Get all of those things into one place (a physical inbox, a paper list, or an online tool).
2. One at a time, go through each item and make the following decisions ("the four Ds" in GTD lingo):
   A. **Do it:** If doing it will just take you a minute or two, get it done now so you can stop thinking about it.
   B. **Defer it:** If it will take more than a minute or two, decide when you will have time to do it or when it is due, then make note of that in your calendar, planner, or to-do app and don't think about it until the day you've assigned yourself to actually work on it. If it's nonurgent and something you want to do eventually, but not at a particular date, assign it as "someday/maybe" and check that file occasionally when you're looking for things to do.
   C. **Delegate it:** If someone else is working on it or could take it off your plate, assign it to them. If it's something that needs to come back to you,

put it in your "waiting on" folder or list with the date you need it back or will check back on it, then forget about it until then.

D. **Delete it:** If it's not important or was a piece of information you just wanted to know, archive it. If you can delete it and be done with it forever, go for it. If it needs to be saved for the future, put it in a reference folder that you can come back to at any time but that doesn't get your active attention.

3. If something in the inbox you're processing isn't a single activity, but instead is a multipart project, break that project down into discrete components using the previously discussed project management methodology and follow that methodology with each subtask of the project.

Using this model will tame your chaos and give you focus in your day to know you're working on the right things at the right time and accomplishing the things you need to.

Inevitably, other needs are going to come up throughout the day (and every day). As much as you can, focus your time and energy on working those into your system too.

GET A QUICK WIN

We've known far too many lawyers who have hundreds (or even thousands) of emails in their email inbox. This is unnecessarily overwhelming and chaotic, and there's a straightforward fix.

One of our favorite productivity hacks is the Inbox Zero system, popularized by Merlin Mann (Lawyerist Podcast #175).

Here's the basic concept: your inbox should just be an inbox. It's not a storage space. To use your inbox effectively, you need to file the emails in it into the places they actually belong. Nobody should have an inbox overflowing with emails. The Inbox Zero system allows you to treat your inbox as an inbox that can be processed and emptied regularly.

To get to the ideal zen state of inbox zero, you'll need to set aside some time on your calendar to do some initial cleaning. After that, it can just become a daily habit.

Here's the basic process:

1. Create email folders in Gmail or Outlook or whatever you use just like you would create file folders for paper, with different folders for cases, finance, HR, marketing, or whatever makes sense for your practice.

2. Also create folders or tags or use stars (or whatever works best for you) to note "Waiting On" emails that you need a response from someone else and "Important" emails that need to have an action or response but will take more than a minute or two to do.

3. Take a first pass at your inbox and delete or archive any emails that don't need your attention (old stuff

that doesn't matter anymore, spam, informational emails that you've now been informed about, etc.)

4. File emails that belong in folders (bank statements, case records that don't require action or response, etc.)

5. File emails as "Waiting On" or "Important."

6. If done right, what remains should just be emails that require a short response. Go through and do that, then file or archive them.

7. Make a habit of processing your inbox this way on a regular basis, checking your "Waiting On" occasionally, and otherwise only working out of your "Important" folder.

8. Inbox zero!

Savvy readers may notice that inbox zero is essentially the email version of the GTD methodology. This is no coincidence!

MOST IMPORTANT TASKS

The GTD model can be supplemented with a "most important tasks" (MITs) framework. Here, you take all of the things that GTD says need attention, select the three that are *the most important* to complete that day, and separate them out from the rest of your to-dos. Your process each day, then, is to get the three most important things done (often by scheduling them into your calendar or by starting only with them first thing in the day). Then you can turn your attention to doing as many of the other not-most-important things as you can.

Combining GTD and MITs will capture everything that needs your attention and help you clearly prioritize your limited time and capacity.

This basic productivity practice will make a tremendous difference in your day-to-day life, and it works with most other personal productivity methods. Every day, every week, simply decide on the three things you can or should be doing, and then keep them front and center. Maybe that means placing those three to-dos at the top of your project management system, or maybe it means writing them down on an index card and putting it by your computer monitor. At the end of the day, once you've completed your three to-dos—and especially if you've completed more—give yourself a high five or a pat on the back because you just created a win.

YOU'RE ALREADY A MASTER PROJECT MANAGER

In legal representation, lawyers are essentially project managers, effectively moving their clients and cases through the system. Most lawyers are very good at this process, and yet for some reason, when it comes to applying the same mindset to their practice, they don't give other processes the same respect they deserve.

Any successful law firm is also a successful business. Whether you're managing a case, your billing process, or a business development initiative, it's important that you learn to approach your work in the same way.

The approaches laid out in this chapter will help you do that. By learning to create basic systems and procedures for your firm, establishing an effective project management system, and improving your personal productivity, you will discover that peace of mind is possible.

And that's the goal. Law firms don't need to be chaotic. They can get large volumes of complex work done in organized, calm, and deliberate ways by following a few practices. When you know what tasks you need to be working on and how you're going to complete them, not only will you be more effective but you'll be a lot happier doing them.

If everything is a priority, then nothing is—and nothing will get gone. Define your processes, find a system that works for you, and then prioritize what needs to get done.

If you go through this process and you realize that you can't get it all done on your own or with your current staff, then it's time to ask some bigger questions. Do you need to hire more staff? Are you able to outsource? Is there a way to change your procedures so that you can delegate better?

MORE RESOURCES

We've put together a set of free tools, templates, and worksheets designed to help you with your firm's systems and procedures. You can download them at lawyerist.com/roadmap/resources.

CHAPTER 11

TECHNOLOGY

Remember how we promised at the beginning of this book that it isn't a book about technology and then we followed up with a chapter on robots and artificial intelligence? Well, this still isn't a book about technology, but here's a chapter all about it!

We don't talk so much about technology because we think it's cool (though often it is) but because it's important. Our expectation isn't that lawyers who read this book all come away fascinated by tech, becoming early adopters of every new gadget and tool. In fact, for the majority of lawyers, that would be a huge waste of their valuable time.

Our expectation is, however, that all lawyers who read this book leave feeling like technology is important and have developed or deepened a genuine curiosity about how it can be used to improve their work.

The age of Luddite lawyers is over. Period.

We know how harsh this sounds, but we're going to take a hard line on this one: proud Luddites have no place in law. Every practicing lawyer must have at least a base level of technology competence. That said, we understand the difference between the proud Luddite and the bewildered adopter. The former wears their ignorance as a badge of honor, while the latter gives tech their best shot—they just rarely see the results they hoped for.

We may not make any friends saying this, but we have zero tolerance for those who are unwilling to learn, explore, and be curious. For those who *are* willing, for those who *are* trying to find the right tools but simply feel stuck, know two things:

· We have nothing but love and respect for you.
· We wrote this chapter specifically for you.

Learning a new skill takes time. It's okay if you're not there yet. You weren't a good lawyer when you first graduated law school, so why should you be good at new software the first time you try it?

In this chapter, we're going to teach you how to develop the mindset and the literacy to use technology to your firm's advantage. First, we'll clear the air with a discussion of some common tech misconceptions. Then we'll go over some systems, tools, and processes you need to have in place at your firm. Finally, we'll share best practices for acquiring the knowledge you need to be a successful tech adopter.

This isn't optional. To be a good lawyer in the twenty-first century—even to be a mediocre one—you *need* these basic competencies.

TECH ADOPTION ISN'T WHAT YOU THINK

Technology is a strategy—or at least a tool that supports strategy. You don't pursue technology for its own sake. You pursue it because it makes you a better lawyer.

For instance, we know a criminal defense attorney in Atlanta who has been paperless for years. When she heads to court, tech bag in tow, she uses her tech to unleash such polished and compelling presentations in the courtroom that prosecutors often offer her clients better deals on the spot. They're terrified of going up against her in front of a jury because they know the kind of show she will put on.

Many of us believe that being tech savvy means being some cyberpunk master hacker, slouching over our three-screen setup and watching lines of code scroll by like we're in *The Matrix*. And just like our *Matrix* reference, that perspective is pretty dated.

Tech-savvy lawyers don't obsess over law practice software. They identify a problem, identify the tools that can solve it, and use those tools to become better lawyers.

One lawyer we know, Eric, is tech-enabled but tool-minimized. The value in Eric's work happens when he meets with his clients and assesses each of their cases. To do his job well, Eric spends a half-hour to an hour prepping to meet with his clients, thirty minutes advising his clients, and then whatever time it takes to prepare for the hearing. In order to accomplish those needs, all Eric needs on-hand is some paper and a tablet. The rest of the work is done through remote assistants, law partners, or outsourced paralegals.

Eric is an example of a tech-enabled lawyer, but it's also worth pointing out what he's not:

- **Tied to a computer.** Eric's value does not involve being tethered to a desk typing on a computer. He has decided that work can be more effectively performed by other people.
- **Tech support.** Any time you spend configuring technology is time wasted. That's the work of an IT professional, not a legal professional.

That's the kind of lawyer we're going to help you become in this chapter. By building a system that effectively uses technology, you can spend your time using your skills as an experienced lawyer in the field.

To help you build that system with confidence, we've broken down the rest of the chapter into the following categories:

- Workflows, systems, and tools.
- Going paperless.
- Data security, threat assessment, and client privacy.
- Training and tech competence.
- Going mobile.

You don't have to be a computer geek to be tech-savvy in business. All you need is an approach to technology that works for your firm. The platforms available today are more user-friendly than you think.

WORKFLOW MINDSET

Good project management and workflows (which we discussed earlier in chapter 10) aren't just about whether they work, but about whether they can make you more efficient. For instance, every firm has to deal with client data. First you collect the data, either manually or using a web form. Then you transfer that data into your project management software. You could do it yourself, but that takes time. Alternatively, you could have your intake specialist do it, but their time is better spent at more high-level tasks.

Instead, you could automate the process. Software is currently available to help your firm in a variety of areas:

- Scan numbers into automatically recognized fields.
- Plug that data directly into your case management software.
- Connect your forms so they work together.
- Conduct due diligence and electronic discovery.
- Scan and categorize documents.

It takes a lot of time and effort to hire lawyers, paralegals, or other staffers to do this kind of work—time that could be spent working on the less rote and more human-focused aspects of your business. Besides, chances are the technology would do the job more accurately than people would anyway.

Think constantly about where you can employ technology to replace your current systems or free up your labor. Every time you examine your systems, procedures, and projects, ask yourself if technology could make any stage of the process more efficient. When approached correctly, automation is your friend.

HOW LAWYERIST DOES IT:
SOFTWARE BUYING PROCESS

For over a decade, lawyers have looked to our team for advice on which software and services they should buy for their practices.

Our long-standing relationships with hundreds of vendors give us a wide and deep perspective on the purchasing decisions firms make every day. As we've now mentioned a number of times in this book, too many small-firm lawyers make decisions about their practice based on the crowd-sourced precedent of the firms around them, rather than figuring out what's the best solution for their firm. Too often in bar association listservs or in our own online community, we hear lawyers ask, "I'm considering buying X. Who here likes X?" We understand the instinct to try to save decision-making time and reduce the risk of a wrong decision by getting outside confirmation that you're making the right decision. But this approach—getting advice from people who aren't trying to solve your same problems and aren't given the context of what your ideal clients uniquely need for the service you're trying to design for them—isn't the best way to find the right tools for you.

Instead, we recommend—and follow—the following four-step approach to making major purchasing decisions:

Step #1: Start with Goals, Not Features

When we're beginning the process of buying new software or services for Lawyerist, we don't start by comparing features lists. We start with an assessment of the goals we're trying to accomplish with this new purchase. We create a short needs analysis document tied to our goals for the company. This needs analysis then leads to a beginning list of core features our solution must have.

Knowing where you are planning to take your firm in the future will give you clarity around your core needs but also the subtle differences in user interface, workflow, and other features.

Step #2: Future-Proof Your Criteria

Most of the software or service purchasing decisions we make are with the goal of them being three- to five-year (or more) decisions, so it's important that we don't just think about our current goals and needs but also spend some time thinking about longer-term potential future needs.

As we mentioned in chapter 2, there are a variety of big trends driving change in technology and we try to think about ways those trends tie to our long-term strategic plans and the tools we use. This gives us a better sense of which solution will grow with us and can help us identify additional features we don't currently need but anticipate wanting or needing in the future.

Step #3: Narrow Down to a Few Finalists

Once we have a clear idea of our short-term and future needs and goals, it's time to do some narrowing down of possible solutions.

Our list of feature needs will vary from those of our peers. This is why crowd-sourcing our purchasing would be a risky path. So while decisions have different needs, here are some features we almost always consider:

- Security protocols (encryption, standards, audits).

- Mobile access (smartphone apps, mobile web interface).

- Design, interface, and ease of use so we can get buy-in from our team.

- The vendor's demonstrated commitment to ongoing development.

- The likelihood of the vendor's longevity and support.

- Ease of transitioning in or out of the software (import/export).

- Full initial cost and likely future cost (setup, consulting, training, additional users).

- Ability to add additional features (APIs, third-party integrations, paid up-sells).

With our list of requirements, we compare the features of vendors in the marketplace to narrow down to at least two, no more than four, finalists to evaluate in depth.

On Lawyerist, we've created a variety of software and services review portals and recommendation tools to help you do this for free, available at lawyerist.com/reviews/.

Step #4: Ask the Hard Questions and Do a Test Drive

Now that we've picked our finalists, we demo the software or reach out to the service provider to understand specifically how it addresses our set of requirements—and to get a feel for working with it.

We take time during our trial period to actually use the tool as we would if we adopted it—running a real case or project through it—and to assess which interfaces and workflows we prefer using so we also know which one we like best.

At this point, we have a clear long-term plan for our goals, understand which vendors offer the features we need, and are clear on which we like using the best. Now we are ready to buy!

GOING PAPERLESS

Some lawyers object to going paperless because they're scared of technology. But that's a horrible excuse. Law firms *need* to be paperless.

It's fine to print out documents when you need them, but your primary authoritative file should be paperless. Create a system that allows you to scan, save, and store documents without creating unnecessary paper copies.

Start digitizing everything that comes into your firm. Yes, that means that you'll need to scan and file every bit of important paper documentation that comes into your office, but the advantage is you only have to file everything once. Once a document is filed, it's filed; you simply navigate to that file on your computer and open it. Because you don't remove it from a folder like you would with paper, the time you'd spend refiling is gone. You aren't wrestling with manila folders or two-prong binders or looking for files that have gone missing.

Not only do you save time, but you'll save space in your office since you no longer have to archive massive files. Sure, you may decide that it's important to save hard copies of certain files. For instance, if you're an estate planner, you may want to save a hard copy of your client's will. We get it, but here are a couple things to keep in mind:

- **Make a digital copy anyway:** If you have a decent and inexpensive printer, printing out a copy takes the same amount of time as scanning and printing it. It's essentially the same activity; the difference is that you only have to scan a document once. After that, you can print out as many copies as you want.
- **Only print what you need:** You may want a copy of your client's will, but you don't need a copy of their entire file.

One thing to keep in mind when going paperless: it's still important to have a document destruction policy. Decide what to do with your files after you're done working with a client.

DATA SECURITY AND THREAT MODELS

A threat model is a way of thinking through the threats to your firm's information, which includes your clients' data and communications. This isn't just a good idea to do. Since 2003, the American Bar Association (ABA) has mandated it; according to Comment 8, Rule 1.1, lawyers must be technologically competent, which includes staying up to date on the risks and benefits of technology.

Even if your state bar association hasn't adopted that comment yet, that doesn't mean you have a free pass to be a tech Luddite. When the ABA released that comment, they clarified that it was already in the rules. Technology competence *is* professional competence— and part of that professional competence includes being able to effectively protect all your data and client communications.

CLIENT PRIVACY

As a lawyer, it's your job to protect your clients' sensitive information from interested parties. If your firm faces a credible threat to your clients' information, you need to try and do something about it.

So what might such a threat look like? It's not always what you think. Consider the cleaning staff that access your office, for instance. If you're in the habit of leaving piles of sensitive client-related information on your desk, you need a confidentiality agreement with your cleaning service. Even if someone in your firm gathers every file and locks it away at night, a confidentiality agreement is still a good idea.

Another unlikely threat is your kids. When waiting to get served at a restaurant, many parents hand their smartphones off to their kids to keep them occupied. If that phone has attorney-client information on it (which is likely), your kid could inadvertently do something to harm your client—not intentionally, of course. In the same way you might accidentally butt-dial someone, your kids might accidentally answer or forward an email.

As a third example, imagine that you left your laptop unattended at a coffee shop, or that you connected to the shop's free Wi-Fi without a virtual private network (VPN). What if someone picks up your laptop, or what if someone is using a packet analyzer to read your emails through your unsecured connection? In either case, the magnitude of the harm is potentially huge. Anybody could be stealing your client's identity or acquiring black-mail fodder.

These are all just basic considerations when considering how to protect your clients' privacy. Breaches like the ones we discussed here come less from malicious third parties and more from negligence. Now, imagine what might happen if an interested party is actively interested in accessing and exploiting your data.

ATTACKS

We don't want to sound alarmist, but the fact is that whatever information you have is at risk of being attacked and accessed by a malicious hacker or opposing party. Over 20 percent of law firms report a data breach annually.[13]

---

13   David G. Ries. "2018 Cybersecurity." American Bar Association. January 28, 2019.
       https://www.americanbar.org/groups/law_practice/publications/techreport/
       ABATECHREPORT2018/2018Cybersecurity/

One type of attack is opportunistic intrusion. In this case, hackers skim the entire internet looking for vulnerabilities. They might blast out email addresses or make robocalls to thousands of people asking questions designed to compromise their networks and give away their credentials. Opportunistic intruders have no particular target. They're just looking for the people who haven't locked their front door. As long as you use basic precautions like good passwords and VPNs, you can limit your vulnerability for opportunistic intrusion.

The second type of attack is targeted hacking. In this case, someone is out to get you or your client. Provided that person is sufficiently motivated, they'll probably find a way in. In that case, you need to consult a security professional and take serious measures to protect your information.

So who may be trying to attack your system? Here a few examples:

- **Spouses.** In the event of a separation, a jilted spouse may want to get into your client's computer. If they're still living in the same house and they know enough about your client to guess their password, that's dangerous. As a lawyer, it's your responsibility to talk to your client about how to avoid those types of threats. This may sound obvious, but sometimes the obvious is the most easily overlooked.

- **Employers.** If a client's employer owns the computer that your client uses to communicate with you, they can easily gain access to whatever information you and your client have shared. Take serious measures to protect your client's information.
- **Businesses.** Say you're representing an American company that has significant trade secrets. If they're going to China, you need to have some serious conversations about how to avoid leaking that data into the Great Firewall.

The way you react to any one of these threats depends on the situation. In the next section, we'll explain how a threat assessment can help you determine your next steps.

CONDUCTING A THREAT ASSESSMENT

The ABA states that you must use "reasonable efforts" to protect your client communications. So, while putting in no effort at all would be negligent, the degree of effort you *do* invest depends largely on the risk.

That's where your threat model comes in. A threat model forces you to think through the various potential threats to your client files and your attorney-client communication. With this model, you can decide which threats to act on and think of a plan to alleviate or avoid them.

To build a threat model, start by asking the following questions:

- What are the risks to our clients' data?
- How likely is each threat to occur?
- What are the potential consequences?
- What's an appropriate measure to take given that risk?
- What would classify as a reasonable effort?

Once you've determined the likelihood and magnitude of the potential harm, you can then determine what steps you will take to counteract the threat. The solution could be as simple as blocking your kids' access to your phone. Whatever the case, the bottom line is this: if you're not making a reasonable effort to protect your clients' sensitive information, you're potentially in violation of ethics guidelines. And make no mistake, adding a disclaimer to your communications isn't enough.

Many lawyers think they're being clever by including an email disclaimer regarding privacy, data security, and confidentiality. These disclaimers give lawyers a false sense that they're doing something good. In reality, such a disclaimer does almost nothing to ensure the security and privacy for their clients. We need to be thinking about these concepts more carefully and treating them with the seriousness they deserve.

GET A QUICK WIN

Here are four basic data security no-brainers to help you start to keep your data protected:

- **Encryption.** Every device you use should use file encryption. If you're on a Mac, enable FileVault. If you're on a PC, enable BitLocker. If you're using an iPhone or iPad, put a password on it, and activate its thumbprint or facial recognition features. Encryption takes seconds. Once you build it into your operating system, everything automatically becomes more secure.

- **Password managers.** Ideally, have a way to securely share passwords between members of the firm. In addition to using a password manager, also use strong and unique passwords. To be clear, 12345 is not a good password. A password manager will randomly generate strong passwords for you.

- **VPNs.** When you're connected to public Wi-Fi, use a VPN or a wireless hotspot. Never connect to the Wi-Fi in a coffee shop, hotel, or airport without a VPN. They cost next to nothing.

- **Two-factor authentication.** Create a little extra security for your key accounts. Wherever your clients' information lives, use two-factor authentication to access it. This could be your management software, accounting software, or whatever software you use to access email. Both Microsoft Office 365 and G Suite offer free two-factor authentication features.

TRAINING AND TECH COMPETENCE

We can't stress this enough: You *need* to be competent at technology. It's simply too important to your client service.

The simple version of this conversation goes like this:

- Figure out what you aren't good at it.
- Get good at it.
- Take as much time on this work as you would on researching your next case.

We're not trying to pick on you or any other lawyers. The simple truth is that most of the tools in most lawyers' offices aren't fully understood and are therefore used poorly. Not only does this affect the quality of your work, but it also affects your efficiency—which, if you're billing hourly, essentially means you're stealing from your client.

To illustrate what we mean, let's use a lawyer's constant companion: Microsoft Word. Say you're drafting a contract, and you need to add a provision between section 1.2.1 and section 1.2.2. Once you insert this new provision, do you manually have to renumber all of section 1.2? Or do you know how to use Word's numbering function correctly?

If you answered the former, first off, thank you for being

honest. We know there's a lot of you out there. Research shows that many lawyers take *four times as long* to complete tasks that involve basic technology like Word and Excel.

Second, we hope you didn't bill the client for that time. Your job was to build the document properly in the first place, not manually renumber every time you have to make edits. Your clients shouldn't pay for you to make changes like this, just like they shouldn't pay you to lick stamps or seal envelopes. Think about it: you wouldn't expect your clients to pay for inefficiencies outside of lawyer work, so why would you expect them to pay for you being bad at technology?

We know of one law firm that kept its client information in two conflicting spreadsheets. The spreadsheets contained different information about the same set of people. The firm was preparing to hire an outside consultant to help them to match up the rows on the spreadsheets and consolidate the data, but fortunately for them, a young lawyer at the firm was able to step in and reconcile all the information using a simple Excel instruction in just a few minutes. None of the older or more experienced lawyers had even this basic competency in their tool kit. Not only would hiring an outside consultant have cost the firm unnecessary time and money, but it would have only been a matter of time before they made a similar mistake again.

If your firm is using software that you don't understand or that you're not proficient at, it's up to you to identify and address that knowledge gap. For now, however, here's some basic advice to save you from hacking your way through all your tasks:

- If you need to keep repeating the same task, find out if there's a built-in function to do it easier. There probably is.
- If your entire firm is struggling with a particular process, figure out how to systematize it or create a workflow.
- If you find yourself formatting tables of authority more than once, learn how to create a master template so that the formatting is taken care of out the gate.
- A truly one-off project doesn't need to be documented in your procedures. If there's a process that your firm will repeat, at least figure out a basic framework for approaching it consistently, and then train everyone on how to do it right.
- As a default, everyone in your firm should be an *advanced* user of Microsoft Word and Outlook, or whatever office suite system you use. It's not enough to have basic Word competence. That's what a seventh-grader has. Expect more out of yourself since you are charging clients as though you are a professional user of these tools.

We get it: as a lawyer, your job isn't to complete complex technological tasks. Neither is it your job to shop for software or image a hard drive. You can hire out tasks like these, but you still need to have a strong baseline of competence so that you know (1) what to hire out, and (2) what to do with the advice you receive.

Start by understanding what technology is capable of. Then distinguish between the tasks you can carry out as a competent person, and the problems that require more complicated and extensive solutions. Chances are, the tools to effectively run your business already live within your walls. It's your job to understand those tools and unlock their potential for your firm.

GOING MOBILE

Your practice shouldn't be tied to your desk. As a lawyer, you sometimes need to access your files and client information from elsewhere.

This means that your data should live somewhere besides your desk, your computer, or your server (if you have one). If you haven't already, it's time to migrate your data to a cloud-based storage solution like Google Drive, Dropbox, or Office 365. This can feel risky at first, but the truth is that cloud-based platforms are more reliable when it comes to backup, recovery, security, and syncing.

Mobile devices like smartphones, tablets, and laptops haven't just made going mobile a good idea but a necessity. You may not go to court, you may not even work remotely at all, but we're willing to bet that you check your work email from your phone every now and then.

When you look at it that way, your firm is already at least somewhat mobile-enabled. Anyone who checks their smartphone outside of the office technically works remotely—and let's be honest, almost everyone does it. Your job then is to make sure you and your team are approaching mobile computing effectively, efficiently, and safely.

Even if your firm is still desktop-focused and you have server-installed software, first, consider the future. Our prediction is that remote-first companies will become a global and long-term trend, at which point, managing your data from your office will become a liability.

In a context where almost all law firms now have at least some, if not all, client data accessible remotely from laptops, iPads, and smartphones, it is critical that you establish firm-wide policies for mobile device usage, access, and security settings.

"ADVANCED" IS THE NEW "COMPETENT"

When it comes to the tech conversation, one of the biggest problems we see is that everyone seems to think they're using it effectively. Some are, but many are not.

As much as we beat up on the "proud Luddite" stereotype, most lawyers have at least made inroads in being a truly tech-enabled firm. But many of those same lawyers haven't taken the time to understand the essential considerations of tech adoption, including how to use the tools they've adopted competently.

We are at the point in business and as a culture where remedial tech skills simply aren't enough. Whatever tool you're using for your business, as a highly paid and trusted professional, you probably need to be an advanced user. If you aren't solving problems in an innovative way, you're not thinking like a lawyer should be in the twenty-first century. Besides, if you're not at least minimally tech-enabled, you're going to find the subject of our next chapter, client acquisition, much more challenging.

MORE RESOURCES

We've put together a set of free tools, templates, and worksheets designed to help you with your firm's technology. You can download them at lawyerist.com/roadmap/resources.

CHAPTER 12

FINANCES

"If I wanted to think about numbers, I wouldn't have gone to law school."

Have you ever heard another lawyer say this? Have *you* ever said this? Most likely, the answer is *yes* to at least one of those questions. For a lot of lawyers, just seeing this chapter might fill them with dread.

Our mission is to flip that idea on its head.

Take it from us: you cannot succeed as a business unless you're excited about numbers. We fully acknowledge and respect that, as a lawyer, your primary goal is to deliver a valuable client-centered service and to pay your employees a living wage with benefits (more on that in the next chapter). In order to do that, however, your business has to be profitable—which means you *must* know how the numbers in your business are doing at all times.

In this chapter, we're going to teach you the basics of good financial best practices so that the next time you look at your books, you're filled with anticipation rather than dread. We'll cover the following topics:

- Creating a long-term financial strategy and profitability model
- Creating and using a firm budget
- Maintaining access to sufficient capital and cash flow
- Getting basic financial controls in place
- Monitoring your financial KPIs and metrics
- Implementing client-centric payment tools to collect the fees you're due

To get the conversation going, let's begin with your responsibility to your finances as a small-firm owner.

YOUR RESPONSIBILITY

Most lawyers know they need to maintain their firm's finances accurately and responsibly, especially when holding client funds. But we think business owners of future-oriented firms have three other financial responsibilities.

- Pay yourself a market rate for the work you perform.
- Your business should be profitable.
- Your business should be saleable.

Across industries, new business owners will start businesses knowing that they won't make money for the first few years. Not only does the business make no money but neither does the owner, who lives off their savings hoping that eventually all their hard work will pay off. From this mindset, paying yourself is a luxury that you defer for later.

The problem with that approach is that these owners rarely have a clear plan for becoming profitable—and therefore for paying themselves appropriately. They often spend too little time thinking strategically about their firm's finances, possibly hiring an office manager, bookkeeper, or accountant to manage their books and never having their own clarity on whether they are on track toward long-term viability.

At the very least, this creates a company equity problem. Generally, law firms aren't saleable as businesses. When lawyers retire, they may "sell" their law firm, but all that really means is that they're handing over equipment and clients in exchange for some sort of (usually nominal) buyout. Those prices are never in line with what it would look like to sell a business—they're more in line with referral fees or short-term case value.

At worst, it can create a serious liability for your firm. One lawyer we know learned this the hard way when their office manager—who was in charge of the books—suddenly quit their job. On its own, this wasn't an insurmountable problem, but the lawyer soon found out the problem ran much deeper: while the office manager had only just quit her job recently, in effect, she had quit her job nine months ago, when she had abdicated all of her responsibilities. She had stopped depositing checks, paying invoices, or anything!

Had this lawyer had good oversight in place, they would've been alerted to this much sooner.

Unfortunately, stories like this happen more often than you might think. While there's nothing wrong with hiring someone to handle the day-to-day financial work of your firm, that doesn't mean you're off the hook. To understand whether your business is profitable—or even whether your bills are being paid—you have to understand what a healthy business looks like from a financial standpoint. At a minimum, this means competency in the following areas:

- Know how your firm makes money and what that means.
- Read financial reports and understand what the numbers mean and how they work. Identify the right benchmarks for your business, like profitability and some key KPIs and ratios.

Now that we've covered the basics, let's take it from the top.

LONG-TERM STRATEGY AND PROFITABILITY MODEL

Every firm should have a documented long-term financial strategy and profitability model. A healthy business has a written plan to forecast its revenue, expenses, net profit, and cash reserves.

Think about this document as the numbers-based counterpart to your firm's written vision and goals (see chapter 6). In other words, this financial planning isn't done once and forgotten about. Your financial plan should be actively used to manage your day-to-day business.

Part of your financial forecast will be about what your next one, three, and five years might look like. You want to see your potential and the steps it would take to get there. The more ambitious the goal, the more attention you will want to pay to make the numbers work. For instance, say you want to generate twice as much income in the next five years. To get there, you could:

- Add more timekeepers.
- Offer a new service.
- Increase or change your pricing.

On an expense side, think about what that growth will cost you:

- Will you have to hire more people?
- Are you going to outsource to contractors?
- Are you going to need new or different technology to support the services you're offering?
- Will you incur other expenses as part of the process?

Once you start asking specific questions like this, you'll start to see the path forward to making your goals a reality.

SET INTERIM BENCHMARKS

In chapter 6, we encouraged you to create a long-term vision about your career goals for the next five to ten years. Next, also document what short-term steps you will take to reach your long-term goals.

This same approach works for your finances. When creating your firm's long-term goals, it's useful to also create and manage your interim benchmarks. For instance, say your goal is to add $300,000 in revenue over the next three years. That means you need to add $100,000 in yearly revenue to keep on pace. Breaking that down further, you would have to add $8,300 in additional revenue each month.

An extra $8,300 sounds much less abstract—and much

more attainable—than $300,000 in three years. So what can you do to get there? To start, look where you are right now.

For instance, say a typical case value averages about $4,000. In order to generate that additional $8,300 in revenue, you need to add two to three additional clients a month. This is where all that marketing work you did in chapter 11 is going to pay off, because it will allow you to set concrete goals. Here, it's all about conversion rate. If you know that half of the people who contact you become clients, you know that you need at least four new contacts each month.

When you turn your big-picture goals into a series of interim benchmarks, not only do they seem more attainable, but you're less likely to fall behind. For instance, it's much easier to try and land two to three new clients a month than to try and land twenty-four to thirty-six new clients by the end of the year. Without regular short-term benchmarks, you may find that three-quarters of the year have passed already, and you're well below your pace for increasing your revenue.

Naturally, there may be some fluctuations. Depending on your practice area, you may find that you get far more clients in July than you do in November. This is good data to have and something that should be factored into your monthly financial goals.

HOW LAWYERIST DOES IT: PROFIT FIRST AND MONTHLY DISTRIBUTIONS

In Lawyerist Podcast episode #205, we talked with Mike Michalowicz, the author of the great entrepreneurial finance book *Profit First*. The Profit First methodology is meant to force entrepreneurs to rethink the profit model of their business. Despite the potential interpretations of the book's title, it isn't about making profit over all else—it's about building a business that is able to distribute a profit from the beginning rather than "waiting until we're profitable."

The general idea is to flip the traditional business finance framework (Profit = Revenue – Expenses) on its head and instead reframe your business's finances as (Revenue – Profit = Expenses). That is to say, build a firm financial model where you take out your profit first before you spend money on overhead expenses.

The formal Profit First methodology includes a variety of specific calculations, financial accounting systems, and banking suggestions, but the general rule is to figure out how your business can have profit on day one.

At Lawyerist, we've adopted a version of this framework that for us includes one important feature we think all firms could adopt: we pay our owners a minimum monthly profit distribution every month (in addition to our base salaries). Some months, we have more or less actual profit than the company earned, but knowing that we'll receive at least our minimum distribution both gives us the peace of mind that we can always feel profitable and also conditions us to build our budgeting around a core of profit rather than just waiting to see what's left at the end.

WHAT IF I DON'T REACH MY GOALS?

Setting financial goals is part art, part science. We aren't trying to test your fortune-telling skills. Your goals and estimates might be way off. Don't sweat it. Your plan will need to be adjusted over time. In an ever-changing world, your spreadsheet will probably change almost every time you look at it. And that's okay. Setting goals isn't an exercise in box-checking; it's an exercise in truth-seeking. The point is not to do this for its own sake but to do it to learn what's working and how things are going.

CAPITAL AND CASH FLOW

Cash is the oxygen of your business. There are two types of cash needed to survive:

- **Short-term cash flow:** Money to fund your day-to-day operations and pay your bills.
- **Capital:** Money to invest in future growth and innovation. Think of your access to capital as a cushion: risk mitigation in case your circumstances suddenly change. This capital will allow you to invest in order to grow.

If you don't have access to the cash you need to feed your business, you're dead. If you don't have enough capital to overcome changes to your projections and invest in your goals, you won't be able to achieve them. So it's crucial that you have access to what you'll need. Even if you're a profitable business, you could face unexpected challenges. According to LexisNexis, cash lockup (the amount of time it takes between producing the work and being paid for it) averages at 139 days, or about 4.6 months.[14] Few lawyers calculate this nearly five-month delay into their budget projections. Most simply think in terms of client and revenue; five new clients a month equals $8,000 in new revenue.

When that money doesn't arrive on time, even if the firm is doing well otherwise, they suddenly find themselves in a cash flow pinch. How do they pay the bills for the next few months as they wait for that projected revenue to come in?

Traditionally, the answer hasn't been pretty. As the old saying goes, commercial bankers will only lend you money when you don't need it, meaning you're unlikely to get relief there. As a result, many small-firm owners resort to desperate measures:

- They don't pay themselves.
- They fund their business using personal credit cards and SBA loans, which usually require that they leverage their house or other assets to secure the loan.

---

14   2012 Lexis Firm Insight survey. Previously available at: https://www.lexisnexis.com/law-firm-practice-management/documents/Billable-Hours-Survey.pdf.

Neither of these options is pretty, and both are signposts that you're no longer being strategic or forward-thinking in your business. So how do you create a business that always has the cash flow necessary to keep the doors open? First, if your firm has a consistent revenue stream, we recommend that you create a buffer of *at least* two months of operating expenses. These will be used to fund your daily operations during any cash flow hiccups. If you have a contingent-fee practice, or a practice with inconsistent revenue streams, your buffer might be higher. For example, some contingent-fee firms might set aside six or twelve months of operating expenses to weather the time between big settlements.

WHEN IS IT OKAY TO ACCESS CREDIT?

Only look to credit as an option if you have confidence you're on a profitable path. Otherwise, you'll end up in debt. There's a big difference between borrowing when you know you're going to have that money and borrowing when you don't know when the money will come in.

If you can demonstrate this long-term profitability, then we encourage you to access available credit when necessary—if for no other reason than your own personal well-being. When law firm owners aren't able to make their base salary, they can feel depressed, confused, or overwhelmed. While tapping into your credit may mean you're working at a deficit for the month, a lot can be said for the stability it will bring in your life. Living on the whims of whether your clients are paying or not can exact a heavy personal toll.

NO REINVESTMENT

Now that we've talked cash flow, let's talk capital. Just like couples will save for a down payment on a new home, businesses need to save for their occasional big investments.

Say you're buying or leasing a new space, upgrading your infrastructure, or improving your firm's technology. Sometimes you need to invest in new people who will help grow your business. Expect it to take three to six months for employees to be running on all cylinders and be fully up to speed with the inner workings of your firm.

Smart businesses will regularly forecast these expenses by making sure they have access to the capital needed to fund them. Ideally, if you can avoid credit altogether, you'll be better off for it. But there are circumstances where a responsible approach to credit can be helpful, provided you follow two general rules:

1. Avoid expensive financing.
2. Budget for the interest you will pay and have a plan to pay the entire loan back.

Outside of credit, there are other ways to raise capital. One is to reinvest your profit. Many firms distribute any profits to their partners at the end of the year. Because that money is going to get taxed, lawyers would rather have it in their pockets. This is often a mistake. Draining your firm's bank account effectively cuts off your ability to grow, innovate, and improve. It also devalues your business.

A third potential—but rarely used—source of capital is from outside equity investors. Though in the United States and Canada there are strict rules governing "nonlawyer" equity ownership of law firms, there aren't similar rules about outside investment by other lawyers. But that's not to say there aren't challenges with this approach.

1. Most small firms aren't very investable businesses. A lawyer looking to invest their money for a profit has lots of other market opportunities, and very few firms are ready to package an investment opportunity with comparable risk and reward.
2. There is no existing marketplace to match law-firm-investment opportunities with law-firm-investing lawyers.
3. These arrangements still need to properly navigate regulations to manage jurisdictional license requirements and conflict-of-interest concerns, but creative arrangement for client-data firewalls and nonpracticing partnership can solve some of these complexities.

If nontraditional firm investment is interesting to you, we recommend keeping yourself informed. A firm's ability to raise funding is one of the big moving questions in the industry. Many lawyers active in national legal-regulatory conversations are pushing for a path toward non-attorney equity in law firms, and there are reasons to think that hard line may start to come down soon and open up a new path toward investment in law firms.

FINANCIAL CONTROLS

A huge portion of malpractice claims and disbarment come from deliberately or accidentally misusing client funds. Sometimes this is the result of financial incompetence. Most of the time, it's the result of desperation.

Almost all of these cases can be addressed by creating good financial control systems. With good financial systems, a firm's money problems can get caught early on, and potentially negligent actions can be prevented.

Effective financial controls include the following key components:

- Clear segregation of duties.
- Defined roles and responsibilities.
- Written and followed policies for all areas of the firm,

including invoicing, payment processing, recognizing revenue, accounts payable, and payroll.
- All bank statements are reconciled each month.
- Your processes and software create and retain an audit trail.
- Firm limits access to certain financial information and software to authorized personnel.

DOCUMENT YOUR FINANCIAL SYSTEMS

Not only will documenting your financial systems and procedures help protect you from fraud or errors, it can also unearth new strategic opportunities or expose possible inefficiencies that could be improved. If nothing else, it makes hiring and training much easier. When you document your financial controls and the movement of money through your firm, you can hand a new bookkeeper a document as a starting point and let them take over from there.

A well-documented system will also help when applying for a line of credit, selling your business, or seeking malpractice insurance underwriting. A packet of policies, controls, systems, and procedures can go a long way toward encouraging someone to take you seriously. The more you can persuade a lender or potential buyer that you know what you're doing, the more likely you are to be considered a low risk. You might be approved for a loan that you might not have otherwise, which adds huge financial value to your firm.

At the very minimum, document who touches the money that goes in and out of your firm at every stage of your work with a client. Better still, separate out the different parts of those functions so the person who touches the money going in isn't the same person who reports on the money going in. Similarly, the person who reports on money going out should be different than the person who actually sends the money out. With bank account access or software access, you can build in controls to separate people to do those different functions.

For example, if you can separate the actions of picking up checks at the post office from entering them in your accounting software and depositing them in the bank, you greatly reduce the risk of someone stealing or mishandling that money. Similarly, the person who authorizes check payments going out should be different than the person with signing authority. If that person was to cut themselves a check or move a number up or down, it's likely they would be caught.

In a solo firm, lawyers often feel this isn't necessary—you're either going to sabotage yourself or you aren't. But even as a solo lawyer, you will likely occasionally use a part-time bookkeeper. The second you begin working with more than one person, it's important that you create a system to delineate things. The earlier you establish these controls, the easier it will be to bring someone else in.

PAY ATTENTION TO THE MONEY

As we were writing this book, someone defrauded Stephanie and her husband's business by stealing their checking account number, printing their own checks, and making a series of big-ticket purchases. Luckily, Stephanie and her husband were alerted to the problem within twenty-four hours because they were paying attention and actively managing their account. Their money was successfully recovered.

If you're a small business with a tight cash flow, a situation like that could cripple you. Even solo lawyers should actively check and manage the money in their accounts. You never know what could happen to you.

BUDGETS AND KPIS

When you've laid everything out correctly, it's exciting to see how the numbers at your company are driving your success.

There are entire books written on the hundreds of possible law firm finance KPIs. It's easy to get excited about all these different ways to track your numbers, but you probably don't need most of them. Too many people get bogged down in the process of creating data that they never use.

To make your numbers work for you, start small. Narrow your KPIs down to five numbers that you need to understand the health of your business. The more comfortable you get, the more numbers you can add. Maybe the five you thought were most critical won't be as important in a few months.

So how do you determine your starting five? Working with your bookkeeper, use the following process:

- Make sure that you're clear on what your goals and strategies are. These will be unique to your firm and provide the framework for determining what it means for your business to be healthy and on track.
- Determine how those goals and strategies might translate as financial indicators. Try to pick a mix of leading indicators (numbers that help you predict what's coming) and lagging indicators (numbers that tell you what happened).
- Create a process to collect those numbers in an objective way in a regular cadence.

- Use your initial data as benchmarks for your firm's financial health.
- Compare your current numbers to your previous numbers. Notice any good or bad trends happening. Make a note of where you might need to make changes.

Your numbers will probably look different from the numbers of other firms—and there's nothing wrong with that. Every firm has unique goals and strategies, not to mention different financial models and benchmarks for success.

GET A QUICK WIN

If you're not sure where to get started with setting some basic financial KPIs for your firm, you might consider some of the following:

1. Profit as a percentage of revenue

2. Accounts receivable over thirty days

3. Cash on hand in nonclient accounts

4. Labor (salary, tax, and benefits) as a percentage of your revenue

5. Realization rate: percentage of fees actually collected

CLIENT-CENTRIC PAYMENT TOOLS AND METHODS

The Clio Legal Trends Report makes it abundantly clear that small law firms lose a lot of money through their invoicing, payment, and collection processes.[15] Historically, lawyers extend their terms out too long, discount too much, and fail to collect on the invoices they send out. As a result, a huge portion of a firm's projected revenue gets lost.

This is unfortunate, but not altogether surprising. Timekeeping and invoicing aren't things they teach you in law school, and honestly, they're rarely even taught in CLEs.

Running a client-centered business means adopting an invoicing, payment, and collection system that accommodates your clients' preferences. With just a little research, you'll be able to find a software solution that perfectly suits your billing needs. However, it's not just the tools you use, but the process you follow. At a minimum, make sure you're doing the following to help your clients pay their bills:

- No matter your billing method (i.e., hourly, flat rate, etc.), invoices are sent out at a regular, predetermined schedule—at least monthly.

---

15   Clio. "2018 Legal Trends Report." 2018. https://www.clio.com/resources/legal-trends/

- Invoices clearly state the work that was done, with descriptions written to be understood by the client.
- Invoices allow for forms of payment that are convenient for clients. Preferably you offer payment by credit card or automated clearing house (ACH), and those payment options have direct links from your invoices.
- You have a system in place for following up on unpaid invoices.

It's unacceptable to wait six months to invoice a client. The more time that lapses between the work being done and the invoice being sent, the less likely you are to collect that money.

In fact, not only will you leave money on the table, but you're making the experience worse for your clients. Every client wants their interaction with a professional or a service to be as smooth and seamless as possible. Anytime an interaction jars with their expectations, it tars the experience.

When a lawyer is flaky with their invoicing or collections, this detracts from the client's experience. Further, when you treat payment like it doesn't matter, then so will your clients.

We get it: asking for money can be an incredibly uncomfortable experience, but it still needs to be done. No business owner, not even a lawyer, is above it. And you can make it infinitely better by starting the conversation early. When you talk openly about money from the beginning, your invoices won't be a surprise, and neither will customer expectations around payment. Further, if you structure your invoices in a way that's easy to understand and easy to pay, then your clients will be much more likely to pay on time.

While being open and honest is without a doubt your first line of defense, we understand that it doesn't always work. Before tossing your arms up in frustration, however, it's helpful to troubleshoot and experiment.

For instance, you could send out bills more frequently or at a different time of the month.

Questions to consider:

- Do you get paid sooner when you invoice on the fifteenth rather than on the first?
- Does it make a difference if you invoice immediately after closing, or when you wait for the next billing cycle?
- Does it improve your cash flow if you clearly state on invoices that payments are due within twenty-one days?

- What happens if you include credit card payment as an option?
- Would a 20 percent or 40 percent retainer make sense for your client?

No matter what, sometimes you'll need to make those dreaded collections calls. You'll find the experience much easier to stomach if you have a system in place for how your firm will collect money.

One successful option we've seen is to have someone else make the calls. This might seem like ducking responsibility, but the reality is that when many people hear another person's voice that isn't their lawyer's, they're more likely to step up and pay. If you're a solo, consider hiring someone for a few hours a month to make those calls on your behalf. (One attorney we know even hired her mom.)

If you'd like to avoid the collections process altogether, you have some room to get creative. For instance, in Sam's practice, he decided that he had no interest in making collections calls or chasing down delinquent clients. Instead, he decided that he would collect all of his fees up front. Such an approach might not work for firms with a high average case value, but the approach made sense for Sam's practice, and he never had to wait to collect on a single invoice.

IT'S ALL ABOUT PROFIT AND GROWTH

With the right plans and systems in place and a newfound excitement for your firm's finances, you can have a clear path to profit and growth. Crafting a long-term financial and profitability strategy and paying yourself a fair salary will decrease your personal risk. Setting aside money for dips and growth investment will improve your firm's chances of success. Making sure you track your metrics regularly and have controls in place will make sure your funds are safe and you see potential problems before they arise. With all of these systems in place and an invoicing system clients are happy to pay, your finances will be something you're happy to think about.

MORE RESOURCES

We've put together a set of free tools, templates, and worksheets designed to help you with your financial strategy. You can download them at lawyerist.com/roadmap/resources.

---- CHAPTER 13 ----

PEOPLE AND STAFFING

Every firm has a culture and values.

If you show up to the office angry at whoever is in the office, that's part of your culture. If you show up with a box of donuts every Friday, that's also part of your culture. Either you've intentionally designed and built that culture, or you've simply let things develop randomly.

A great firm is a great place for you and your team to work. To create a great place for you and your team to work, you must be committed to hiring team members who align with your vision and values.

A team of people rowing together in the same direction has a clear goal and way to get there. When everyone is in sync and paddling to a rhythm, there's nothing you can't do. That's when you're at your best and most productive.

Deciding on your mission and values isn't just a fun exercise. It's an exercise in pointing the ship and banging the drums for your rowers so everyone can move in the same direction at the same time.

In this chapter, we're going to teach you how to build a team that is all rowing in the same direction. With a little intention and a commitment to fairness, diversity, and transparency, you can create a small-firm culture that reverses the toxic narrative of the traditional law firm that we've alluded to throughout this book. To create a healthier work environment, we must create a firm culture that sees work and one's personal goals in harmony rather than in opposition.

This isn't going to be easy.

For decades, the legal profession as a whole has tossed the work-life balance question right out the window. Even before law school, aspiring lawyers are taught to take pride in how stressful, dysfunctional, and time-intensive their jobs are. Most of us have been conditioned to see law as a grind. We proudly flaunt our work-hard-play-hard attitude. We compete with other lawyers over who can work the hardest or who has the toughest case load. But while it's one thing to aspire to greatness, for many of us, that aspiration has morphed into a pattern of self-destructive behavior.

The negative effect not only on personal health and well-being but on the overall culture and health of the firm, cannot be overstated:

- Traditional law firms are known to make their employees sick and miserable. Lawyers and legal staff often suffer from higher rates of mental illness, stress, and substance abuse than those in other professions.
- Firm owners are rarely focused on being good managers or offering good career paths for the people in the organization.
- Fair compensation and benefits are often taboo topics.
- Compensation is often tied to performance metrics, creating a competitive environment in the firm where team members might even work against each other to maximize their own personal gains.

In this environment, performance suffers. No one gets what they want. We've heard from countless small-firm managers who are constantly frustrated that their employees are not doing what they're asked to do. We know one firm owner whose relationship with his employees is so contentious that he dreads processing payroll because he doesn't think his employees deserve the compensation. In firms like these, rather than addressing the root problem, those in charge instead perpetuate the cycle, demanding more work for less reward and further poisoning the culture well.

That needs to stop.

Such an environment benefits no one. It leads to a higher rate of turnover, diminished productivity, and overall poor performance. A bad culture, aside from the sheer unhappiness and misery it produces, also leads to a bad bottom line. It's simply not good for business.

That's why we believe it's so important that the law firm of the future is also a healthy place to work. When you're intentional about creating a healthy culture where your employees are aligned around your vision and values, not only will you have created a healthy and fun workplace, but you will have created a more independent, productive workforce.

This isn't to say that you'll be able to create some sort of small-firm utopia overnight—or ever. No matter what, employees will still leave, and you'll still need to spend time and money hiring and training new employees. Almost every job, after all, is a stepping stone for another job.

Rather than create a culture of punishment and mistrust worrying employees might leave, why not embrace this fact? Why not build your systems and procedures around helping people develop along their chosen career paths? Any employee prefers an employer who is invested in them. When they see you're interested in their long-term development rather than extracting the most possible value from them for the smallest possible paycheck, they will reward you in a variety of ways. They'll stay longer with your firm, they'll give you better work output, and they'll even gladly become a source for referrals long after they've left.

We've seen the impact a healthy, employee-oriented culture can have both in our own business and in small firms across the country. Granted, with implications for compensation, workload, vacation, hours worked, and supportive services, amongst other things, building this culture takes work. But the benefits of a more engaged, more productive, and above all, *healthier* team is well worth the investment—and it all starts by having clearly defined roles within your organization.

CREATING AN ORGANIZATIONAL CHART

Most law firms build their reporting structures around seniority. There is often little clarity over who manages whom, and in what capacity. Employees simply report to the senior lawyer, and that's as far as the conversation goes.

A written organizational (org) chart can help you lay out the essential functions of your firm. Whether you have one lawyer or a dozen, your firm will have billing, accounting, collections, sales, marketing, and IT functions—everything we've discussed already in our Small Firm Roadmap. By creating a detailed functional org chart, you will be clear on who is responsible for what, who they report to, and how each organizational function fits into the larger picture. This brings clarity not only to you and other managers but also to your employees, who are better able to distinguish between their roles.

In a small firm, we recommend starting with a functional approach to creating your initial org chart:

1. First create a chart based solely on the functions within your firm, not yet noting who in the firm has that role.

2. Start with the leader of the firm (the managing partner, CEO, owner) and note what roles that function needs to play in the organization, which likely includes things like firm vision, overall profit and loss, maintaining firm culture and values, and team management.

3. Then map out the next level of the chart, which is the leadership and accountability for each primary function of your firm. This likely includes at least sales and marketing, legal services delivery, and firm finance and administration. Your firm may divide these functions up differently or have additional import-

ant functions, but as a default, feel free to start with these three. For each of these functions, note the roles and accountabilities for each. For legal services delivery, this might include new client onboarding, case management and success, client experience feedback, and team management.

4. On the next level (or levels) of the chart, add in any other functional roles in the firm. These might include roles like lawyer, paralegal or case manager, and intake or client service. Note the roles and accountabilities for each of these functions.

5. Once you've mapped out all of the functions in your firm, then go back in and add names to each box. Remember our "management by committee" discussion from chapter 1. Be very careful about having more than one person with the same accountability. (It's fine to have multiple lawyers with similar roles, obviously, but it's best to only have one in charge of a particular function.)

6. As you do this, you may find that there's no one assigned to a particular function. In that case, it's likely you need to temporarily put yourself into that role to make sure it's accomplished.

This exercise is likely to lead to some realizations that some accountabilities in your firm don't have a single clear leader, or that someone (often you) is wearing way too many hats to effectively accomplish the work that needs to get done. Alternatively, you might realize you have the wrong person in a current seat or not enough staffing for a particular function.

Such realizations are valuable for firms to learn about their businesses. For instance, firm managers often find themselves wondering whether they should hire a paralegal or an attorney. Once you've mapped your current team and the needed functions of the firm, you'll likely have clarity over your greatest areas of need. What do you need that person to do? If you need help with researching and filing, hire a paralegal. If you need help representing clients in court, hire an attorney.

The value of such clarity can't be overstated. Often, firm owners or managers don't know what they're looking for when looking to add personnel. They begin the interview process blind. Then they hire the first "great person" they find and hope they can figure out a role for this person once the dust has settled.

If you're running a big business or a large law firm, this approach *could* work. If you hire a talented person who is a good culture fit, you may be able to bounce them around different roles until you've found the best job for them.

In a small firm, however, you might not have that luxury. While you want to hire great people, you need great people who can fulfill the right role for you. That competency element is critical. An org chart will help you make better decisions throughout your hiring process and better match your hires to suit your business needs.

This isn't just good for you but also for your employees. Too many new hires feel lost, unsure about what's expected of them. When you're clear on what you're looking for and how they fit in with the rest of the organization, *they're* clear on that too.

HIRING FOR CULTURAL FIT

The earlier and more often you talk about your firm's culture, the better the hiring process will be for everyone. Of course, to hire people that fit your culture, you first need to figure out what your culture is. Once you're clear on this and have built your vision and values into the workplace, find a meaningful way to articulate your culture and share it both in your job posting and early in the interview process.

The more you hide your culture in your job description, the more applicants you'll have to filter through. Further, you'll be more likely to take a chance on someone who isn't a good fit. They might be tactically and technically perfect, but if they're a cultural outlier, it won't work out in the long term.

Your selection process will go more smoothly from start to finish when you can identify and reject applicants who aren't a good cultural fit for you. In turn, you'll have more room to focus on your interview process and to find someone with the right skills for the job.

Let's take a moment to break this process down in a little more detail.

DEFINING "CULTURE"

Before we get into the *how*, let's make sure we're clear on what we're talking about when it comes to culture. After all, "culture" has become somewhat of a buzzword in modern business books, each with a slightly different definition.

First, let's start with what it's not: "culture" does not equal homogeneity, and here it has nothing to do with race or ethnicity. While it's important for your new hires to fit the business culture of your firm, this doesn't mean that they will be exactly like you—in fact, they *shouldn't* be. That's not what good culture is.

The best companies deliberately hire staff members with a variety of competing perspectives and ideas. In order to be stretched, you need to surround yourself with people who don't always keep you comfortable. In life and business, we should be learning new things and seeing situations from different angles and perspectives.

Now, let's move on to our definition of what it *is:* Work culture is what it's actually like to work at your firm—the result of the many interactions between team members. Through these interactions, culture develops from the bottom up, not from the top down.

This means that, whether their culture was intentionally nurtured or not, all firms have one—and everyone is responsible for it. While a firm's leaders are instrumental in setting the tone by establishing the firm's vision and values, they can't declare the organization's culture and make it so. For your culture to reflect your values, the people who work in the organization need to live and drive those values themselves. For this reason, it is essential that your firm hires for cultural fit.

JOB POSTINGS

The way you advertise for roles in your company is important. Aside from identifying the role and the skills you need, make sure to include your firm's mission and values. Talk honestly about the attributes you need for someone to be successful and aligned with the culture you're trying to create. Don't be afraid to ask for a non-standard cover letter or statement to give applicants the opportunity to explain why they would be a good fit for you.

Remember, the purpose of a hiring process is to weed through the masses and find the best fit for your firm. The hiring process is about trying to eliminate people. Out of a hundred candidates, you have to find the *one person* who is the best fit for you, and vice versa.

The job description is your first opportunity to do that. Again, be creative here and describe in detail what you do and what it means to work for your firm. Too many firms just use the same plain language as everyone else. This won't do you any good. Get rid of it.

As an example, we once worked with a small firm that was advertising for a job. In the description, they included two unique details:

- Applicants must appreciate a dry sense of humor.
- Applicants must be open to a dog-friendly office, as they had three or four dogs in the office every day.

Out of hundreds of people who responded to the ad, less than five addressed those two points in their cover letter. Ultimately, the firm hired the woman who talked about her love of rescuing and fostering dogs. By being specific about who they were and what they were looking for, this firm was able to find the person who was the best overall fit for the firm.

Another firm we worked with advertised for a person to be open to occasional foul language in the office. The firm represented high net worth individuals embroiled in divorces, affairs, and sex scandals—which were all spoken about openly as a natural course of work at the firm. The job ad made it clear that applicants should be open to hearing multiple F-bombs daily and that they should only apply if they could see themselves working in that sort of firm. A potential candidate who would be offended by that language (or offended by the mention of it in the posting) wouldn't be a good fit for that firm, so it's a great tool for quickly finding the people most likely to work well with you and your team.

INTERVIEWING

Interviewing is a skill. Despite what people think, there *is* a great way to interview people. If the interview ends with you liking the candidate and thinking they're a nice person, that's great. But that alone isn't enough to know whether that person will be successful in your organization.

As an interviewer, try to gain specific information that will help you determine whether a candidate will be good for your firm. This begins by changing your mindset. Too many lawyers, law firms, and employers approach hiring as a way of finding someone *good enough*, rather than someone who's *amazing*. The problem with this mindset is that if you're focused on hiring people who are only good enough, then your firm, too, will only be good enough.

If you want your firm to be amazing, you must hire amazing people. This is why it's so important to not only define your vision and values but also to define the job you're hiring for. Once you've carefully defined those standards, be unyielding in searching for them when interviewing candidates. If you interview fifty people for a job and none of them fit, don't hire the person who was good enough—don't hire anybody. Reconsider your job posting and where you're advertising and try again.

Also, reconsider the interview process itself. By changing the way we ask questions, we can get better information. We're big fans of behavioral interview techniques, which are a way of asking questions about past performance as a way of gauging future performance. If you're interested in learning about this type of interviewing, we recommend tracking down a copy of *Who* by Geoff Smart, which offers a great framework for conducting successful interviews.

PROVIDING FAIR COMPENSATION

Compensation can be a difficult issue in a small law firm. Because lawyers generally aren't taught how to run a business, they're generally unsure of how to approach the question of employee compensation. Unsure of what else to do, they adopt the default compensation model found at most law firms—a model that doesn't do anyone any good.

Law firms are traditionally built around the "rainmaker" model: whoever brings in the most clients and owns the most client relationships is the highest-valued member of the firm—financially, culturally, and otherwise. In business terms, this rainmaker is essentially the firm's lead salesperson, and they guard their client assets carefully.

In such a system, whoever owns the client relationship is incentivized to hold on to that relationship. This means that they typically don't want their clients to meet or spend any meaningful time with other lawyers—even other lawyers in the same firm. Nevermind that someone else in the firm might be better equipped to handle the case or offer a unique perspective; this exclusive relationship must be protected at all costs.

This has resulted in perverse thinking about compensation that has permeated the entire industry, whether explicitly or implicitly, all the way down to law school.

Such an institutionalized practice becomes hard to avoid. Even if you recognize something as a poor model, it's hard to rethink the only thing you've ever known.

So, when most lawyers set out to start their own firms, they structure their own compensation models in the same broken way, conflating compensation and revenue as causally linked. In other words, if the firm lands a $4,000 client, the question immediately becomes a matter of what percentage of that fee goes to whom. This in turn leads to a zero-sum competition between the lawyers in the same firm, who end up fighting between each other to decide how to divide revenue so that they get the bigger piece of the pie.

Suffice it to say, that's not the compensation model we're advocating for here. Not only does it contribute to a toxic work environment, but there's also a better way.

RETHINKING FAIR WAGES AND INCENTIVIZATION

In his popular business book *Drive*, author Daniel H. Pink explains the difference between incentivizing employees with intrinsic and extrinsic motivators. Part of his research shows that almost all people have a threshold salary that is "enough" to be paid to no longer worry about money. In the simplest terms, if you reach or exceed that threshold, whatever it might be, then you are compensating that employee fairly. (To be clear, this isn't to say this "enough" amount should be their compensation cap, just that there is a fair amount at which employees can focus less on extrinsic rewards and be fully dedicated to the intrinsic rewards of good work).

Fair compensation, then, begins with a fair wage. Make sure that everyone in your organization, especially the partners, are paid a regular and fair salary that stops them from worrying about whether they can pay their bills or not. After that base salary, then you can start to think about other benefits, such as profit distributions and incentivization. But as you go down the road of structuring incentives, make sure that you're designing a system in which everyone in the organization can feel happy, healthy, and motivated to provide the best client experience.

Sometimes this won't be through extrinsic motivators, which generally motivate people to think about themselves rather than thinking about providing long-term value. With an extrinsic motivator, they're only conditioned to think about what *they* can extract from the process—which, for anyone outside of the rainmaker, may not be much.

Imagine that you promise an employee that they will get

a third of all the business they bring in. This may sound like a win-win, where both you and the lawyer share in their success in helping grow your firm, but a commission structure incentivizes them to bring in *any* business, regardless of its fit with your definition of an ideal client or its fit with your long-term goals for growing your practice.

Further, it discourages them from investing in the success of both their coworkers and their firm: employee A would have no reason to care how employee B's clients are faring.

This, of course, begs the question: What kind of firm are you building if your employees don't care how either their coworkers or the company as a whole are doing?

For better or for worse, whatever you're compensating is what you're incentivizing. Your job is to be clear about what behavior you're trying to incentivize and to create a compensation model that suits that goal.

For instance, if you want to incentivize more business into the firm, that doesn't just mean to incentivize the rainmaker who closes the deal. Instead, look at the law firm as a whole system, one with goals and values. In such an environment, business can come from anywhere—a blog, a clever marketing campaign, or even a well-timed follow-up call. Even employees who don't directly bring money in are valuable. A well-trained receptionist with good intake practices is just as likely to make clients feel happy as your senior partner who is part of a business networking group.

Success is achieved when teams work together toward their goals, and your incentivization system should reflect that. Incentivize everyone to work in ways they excel. If you send a socially awkward employee to a networking lunch, that environment will not encourage success. That same employee, though, might write amazing marketing articles that *do* contribute to the overall success of the firm.

FEE SHARING

For years, there has been a rule against lawyers splitting their fees with "non-lawyers." The profession has always sought to be above practices like referral fees with outside vendors, or any other practice where lawyers are incentivized to take on or settle cases against their clients' best interest for alternative compensation. As the common thinking goes, lawyers must maintain their integrity by only taking money from clients when they are acting in those clients' best interests.

While the basis of this rule is valid, the concept that lawyers shouldn't "share fees" is problematic when taken to its extreme of implying that they can never share profits. In fact, it places a firm's other employees at a disadvantage. Firm owners are hesitant to pay these employees any compensation that might look like a bonus because doing so might be seen as unauthorized fee splitting.

For instance, imagine a case comes in with the potential for a big settlement. According to the rules, it would be an ethical violation to offer your paralegal 10 percent of your firm's proceeds for their work. But it should be a different matter entirely to allow employees to share in the overall profits of the firm. In that broader case, there is no direct ethical conflict between the employees and incentives and duties toward any specific client. But because ethics rules become interpreted so broadly that they are no longer connected to their underlying ethical considerations, most jurisdictions impart an overall ban on sharing even overall profits with "non-lawyer" employees.

That's not fair, but fortunately, there are other ways to look at compensation. We're not your professional responsibility advisor, but as far as we can tell, there's no rule against guaranteeing to pay your paralegal a base salary of $65,000 a year and, provided they hit certain non-fee-based KPIs, like client satisfaction or case output, offering them a set bonus every quarter. Such an arrangement should have no implications for fee sharing and provides a financial incentive to employees to help drive goal-connected growth in the firm.

This is one reason we've emphasized KPIs throughout our Small Firm Roadmap. Not only do they help you track what your firm is doing, they also track who is doing the work—and therefore, who should be rewarded for a job well done. If the firm meets its quarterly goals, then everyone benefits. Approaches like this incentivize profirm behavior while promising individual gain. Everybody wins.

To some of you reading this, our suggestion may sound like a rhetorical workaround. We believe there are no fee-sharing legal ethics rules implicated in a compensation model that isn't tied to fees. Any arrangement which isn't tied to fees doesn't implicate fee sharing. But we also acknowledge that certain ethics boards might disagree with us.

If you're at all worried about the ethics of such an arrangement, don't blindly let that worry dictate your actions. Inform yourself. Look up the rules in your jurisdiction. Consult your local ethics authority. Don't take our word for it; do what you need to reassure yourself about your plans.

PAY YOURSELF FAIRLY

Attorneys, including partners, should be paid at a market rate. Period.

If you're an owner or partner of a firm, there are two buckets of money you can make:

- The work you perform for your firm. This compensation should be equivalent to what you'd be paid in the market. This is your salary.
- A return on your investment for owning a business. This is your profit.

Law firms typically conflate these two buckets. In most firms, partners get paid all the firm's profits—in other words, whatever money is left over at the end of the year becomes their "salary."

Our approach is a big departure from this thinking, but it comes with its benefits:

- It will give you as the business owner a more complete picture of the health of your firm. If you can't afford to pay yourself what you'd be paid in the market, this should be a red flag that your business isn't healthy.
- As an owner, you need to understand your true profitability percentage to determine if you're making a good investment in the business. Are you getting a reasonable return on investment? If you pay yourself solely on the profits, you won't know what this number truly is.

At some point in the future, you may want to replace

yourself, sell your business, or hire somebody else to do some of the jobs you're currently doing. Committing to paying yourself your market rate salary now will give you the ability to make that transition one day because your replacement's salary is already in the budget. Not only does this help you and other people understand the true value of your firm, but it helps you understand how to eventually replace yourself.

When you have a brand-new firm, you're still trying to get clients in the door. During the first three, six, or twelve months, it may be impossible to pay yourself consistently, or you may want to reinvest that money into your firm. We get it. After that, though, if your firm is going to be viable, it has to be viable as a regular business.

In other words, once that three-, six-, or twelve-month grace period is over (that period is up to you), it's time to start taking out a regular salary. This is your base compensation. This will do wonders for your psychology. If you let your wages ebb and flow with your business, the financial fear and anxiety that produces will detract from your ability to run the business.

If your business isn't healthy enough for you to regularize base payments to yourself, it's failing, and you'll want to know this quickly. While you can give yourself time to get to that point, you *do* eventually have to get to that point.

PAY EVERYONE ELSE FAIRLY TOO

Once, during a coaching session with Stephanie, a partner at a small firm realized that he had been relying on his wife to do the majority of the firm's marketing, and they weren't paying her a dime in compensation.

His wife had been happy to help—jumping in to make a family's small business work is what spouses do. But that work required a lot of her time and energy. The partner decided he needed to pay her for the value she was providing the business.

Not only was he super excited to pay her, but there were immediate changes:

- Getting paid made her feel great. We often forget how psychologically validating it is to be paid fair value for our work.
- Paying her to set the firm up for the future. Whenever the firm decided to hire someone other than the partner's wife, those marketing costs were already in their budget, and the firm already knew what work it needed to outsource.

Pay everyone—even the spouse who's just happy to lend a hand. If you don't, how can you know the true cost of your marketing or leads if you aren't acknowledging that you pay someone to do marketing or develop leads? Further, how do you know if your business is actually healthy and is making the margins it needs to survive?

The broader point here isn't about what to do with volunteer spouses, it's to remove artifice and misaligned incentives from your compensation structure as quickly as you can. If there's enough work in your firm to require hiring a new associate, there should be enough revenue to pay that associate a market-rate starting salary, rather than bringing in people on spec in an "eat what you kill" model. If there isn't the financial capacity to fairly compensate that new employee from the beginning, then there either isn't actually the workload need for them, or your fee structure and profit margins didn't actually fit in the financial strategy you created in the previous chapter.

Everything that costs significant time, money, and energy should be tracked. That way, your KPIs and your budget will reflect what's happening in your firm, your employees will be happier to be paid a fair wage, and you will know for sure that you're on the right track.

COMMITTING TO DIVERSITY, ACCESSIBILITY, AND INCLUSION

We've spent some time in previous chapters discussing the importance of thinking about diversity, inclusion, and accessibility for your clients and the importance of all of us making sure that the legal services we deliver are broadly available to all people in our communities.

A corollary goal, with the same combination of idealistic and practical justifications, is that we should all think about how we can make our work teams (both attorneys and non-attorneys) supportive of diversity, accessibility, and inclusion.

At the same time that too many minority populations struggle with access to justice, the law firm employment market is also underinclusive. According to NALP's 2018 Report on Diversity in US Law Firms, women, racial and ethnic minorities, the GLBTQ community, and people with disabilities are all underrepresented in the legal profession compared with their representation in the broader population.[16]

As employers in our small firms, we have the ability to work to correct these wrongs. But we also have the opportunity to improve our firms through this work both because more inclusive teams are documented to perform better overall[17] and because a more diverse staff is

---

16 National Association for Law Placement. "2018 Report on Diversity in US Law Firms." January 2019. https://www.nalp.org/uploads/2018NALPReportonDiversityinUSLawFirms_FINAL.pdf

17 Vivian Hunt. "Why Diversity Matters." McKinsey & Company. January 2015. https://www.mckinsey.com/business-functions/organization/our-insights/why-diversity-matters

likely to help you improve your ability to address the huge market opportunity from a more inclusive client base.

Diversity, in other words, is a competitive advantage.

Of course, in the big picture, it's not just about success. It's about impacting both your profession and the world in a positive way. The best way to correct for bias in the legal profession is to correct for that bias in your own firm by hiring and managing with diversity in mind. Of these, the biggest hurdle by far is hiring; for many firms, simply attracting and selecting employees of diverse backgrounds is a considerable challenge.

When hiring, we tend to look for people whose stories match our own—people who know the same pop culture references, who get the same inside jokes, and who have the same hobbies outside work as we do. This can be the trap of not taking a broad view of what culture-based hiring should mean. Homogeneity might seem like a good idea when looking for a good cultural fit for your firm, but it unnecessarily limits the type of people who you welcome into your firm.

The reality is that great employees can come from a variety of places and still be a great work-culture fit. In fact, we would argue that hiring for diversity creates a *better* organizational culture. A variety of stories and experiences (all sharing the same work-engagement values) inside your walls equips you to have better conversations, make harder decisions, and create a marketing message with a broader appeal.

But as many companies have found, you can't just "do diversity" by hiring more women, people of color, or people with disabilities. Throwing a bunch of people with different backgrounds and perspectives and abilities into a firm only works if the team is healthy, meaning everyone feels safe expressing their opinion and knows it is valued.

So diversity in hiring is only one part of the equation. The other piece is taking that diversity seriously once people are on your team and creating a welcoming environment that values each person for their contributions. Whenever possible, it's important that you consider whether you're inadvertently insulting someone or making them feel uncomfortable or out of place.

When it comes to considerations like this, it's often the little things that make people feel welcome—or unwelcome. For example:

· If all of your office parties involve alcohol, do team members who don't drink (for whatever reason) feel welcome and want to participate in those events?

- If some lawyers in your firm like to golf together during work, do team members who don't (or can't) play golf feel like they have the same opportunities for banter, relationship-building, or outdoor breaks from work?
- Are all of your team's nonwork social activities outside of work hours so that only people with flexible home schedules and transportation options can easily participate?

These are just a few small ideas. The point is to check to make sure your firm is working to engage and support everyone.

Committing to diversity, accessibility, and inclusion takes time and effort. You're not going to get it all right at once, and actions speak louder than words in this case. Consistently demonstrating the effort will go a long way in showing that you are truly invested in making your firm a more inclusive and diverse place to work.

FOSTERING STRONG MANAGEMENT SKILLS

As with the development of most business skills, most lawyers have never been trained to manage others. Consequently, they often adopt many of the same horrible, hard-line management practices they witnessed as junior associates.

This "pay your dues" attitude needs to stop.

Just because you had to endure hell when you were coming up through the ranks doesn't mean that your employees should have to as well. We want to make this point especially clear because we've heard from several firm owners over the years whose stated philosophy is, "I had to go through hell, so you have to as well."

A leader with this attitude cannot run a healthy or growth-oriented company. The happier and healthier your team, the better they will treat your clients, and the more money your business will make. Everybody wins.

If you're going to be managing other people, that should be a skill that you actively learn and try to improve just like any other skill that might be an important part of your work.

One of the easiest ways to do this in a small way is to distribute some of that responsibility. The senior attorney does not have to manage everyone else at the firm. Traditionally, law firms structure their org charts and reporting structures so that junior people report to senior people—period. The attitude is that that's not how it should be. But the reality is that anyone in your firm could potentially mentor someone else in the firm. Structure your org chart so that functional people report to the decision-maker in that functional area and that one of the skills a person needs to lead in that role isn't just seniority but includes the ability to effectively manage others.

THE FOUR QUALITIES OF AN EFFECTIVE MANAGER

So what does it take to be an effective manager? In Julie Zhuo's book *The Making of a Manager*, she lays out the three qualities of effective management—*people*, *purpose*, and *process*—and we've added our fourth: *path*.

#1: People

At the end of the day, people want to be cared for as human beings in their jobs. As a leader, your responsibility is to take care of your people. To do this, you have to engage with, talk to, and get to know them. Build a foundation with your team. Be intentional. Schedule sit-down meetings with them. Help each of your employees define their purpose, not just in this one job but in their career. Invest your time and effort into helping make sure that your employees are on a path to reach their career goals and to be successful in their current role in your firm. Whenever problems come up, be ready to coach them.

#2: Purpose

People work with a purpose. To do good work, your team members must see a connection between their work and the firm's larger vision and purpose in the world. Employees also want to receive recognition and gratitude for the work they do.

As a leader, share success stories and connect them with your values. Our leadership team does a great job of recognizing everyone else on the team. Every time we recognize a team member, we explain how they're living our core values.

#3: Process

People want to know they're succeeding, that they're doing their job correctly, and they want their success to be measurable. Give every team member their own set of KPIs. Lay out those expectations in writing. Be clear about their role, their responsibility, and how they'll be measured.

When employees struggle with work quality, or following the firm's processes, circle back to the tools we covered in for systems and procedures in chapter 10.

#4: Path

Your employees should know how their work fits on their career path. If they're an associate, show them a path to partnership.

This shouldn't be a secret. Every employee should have a chance to learn what their career path looks like. Be transparent around what it means to advance in your firm. Give people an opportunity to show up and be their best selves.

In the past, seniority was a black box that young associates were blindly encouraged to chase. More often than not, the people who achieved seniority ended up underwhelmed with what they got. Without a level of transparency, you deprive team members of the opportunity to consider what they do or do not want to pursue.

While transparency is a great way to run a firm and incentivize and educate young associates, you don't have to be an open book. Just be strategic about what you teach lawyers and what you expect their work to look like.

COMMUNICATION

Communication is essential to any business. But while every business communicates between employees, not every business communicates intentionally.

Every team member should know the important things going on in your organization. To facilitate that, every firm should have a structure in place that will allow leadership and management to keep everyone up to date.

Yes, this means you'll have to attend and lead meetings. That said, let's get one thing clear: bad meetings suck. A poorly structured and poorly run meeting is the worst use of time for everyone involved.

So, while we do recommend that you hold some specific meetings, we *don't* recommend that you hold meetings for meeting's sake. An intentional, well-structured meeting is the most effective way to communicate important news, needs, and requests in the least amount of time. We've seen plenty of businesses opt for the shotgun approach to meetings, updating employees with bursts of information throughout the day. While that may be a great way to interrupt people, it's not a great way to communicate important information.

STRUCTURING YOUR COMMUNICATIONS

In any firm, you must make use of different communications strategies to make sure information is flowing through the organization.

First, firm leadership should hold regular meetings, ranging from weekly to monthly. These meetings should have a standing agenda and a fixed cadence and be focused on solving strategic issues within the organization, not with just hearing people talk.

Second, attorneys must have an effective way to communicate with their team on the work of the law firm. In order to serve your clients, you have to be talking about your cases. Email tends to be the default for many firms, but it's often ineffective and scattershot, leading to too many distractions throughout the day.

Stand-Up Meetings

One idea we like is to hold regular "stand-up" meetings with your team members. Often, stand-up meetings are literally what they sound like: During a quick five to ten-minute check-in, team members stand up, discuss their projects for the day with the goal of moving them forward, and then go back to work, never having sat down. These stand-up sessions can be facilitated by a team leader who asks questions like:

- What are you working on?
- How is it going?
- Are there any roadblocks in your way to getting it done?

The purpose of a stand-up meeting is to quickly connect

with your team on the work they're doing, check in to make sure everyone has the necessary information, and answer any questions needed to move their work forward.

Management Availability

Last is the question of the open-door policy. As good managers and leaders, we want to keep our doors open to answer any questions our employees might have. At the same time, we don't want constant interruptions distracting us from getting our work done.

As a solution, you could set a specific office hours period for each day. We've found that if you integrate stand-up meetings into your routine, you will dramatically reduce the need for an open-door policy. With regular stand-up meetings, your team members will know that they have consistent access to your time. That way, if they do have a question, and it's not pressing, they can save it for their stand-up meeting instead of interrupting a heads-down workflow.

HOW DID WE DO?

Are your meetings as effective as they need to be? If not, what can you do to improve them?

After many of our meetings, we ask the participants to

give us a score from one to ten. This isn't to trick our employees into giving us a ten—we're not looking for a pat on the back. We ask for this feedback because we want concrete data on how our meetings are going. If an employee scores a meeting less than an eight, we ask them, "What would it have looked like for the meeting to get a 10?"

Luckily, we have enough trust, vulnerability, and openness that people in our organization aren't afraid to raise issues. We know this because we've experienced it. There was a time when we were giving ourselves really good scores at the end of our meetings. Eventually, we took a step back and realized that we may have been conducting our meetings well enough, but we were also playing it safe and avoiding hard conversations. Our scores were based on the fact that we were dealing with the easy topics well.

It's not the meetings themselves or how they're structured that will lead to openness, honesty, and vulnerability. Instead, it's the way you model these values as you lead or participate in the meeting. Demonstrate transparency, openness, vulnerability, and honesty at the highest levels, and these values will come to define your organizational culture. This can be hard work, but it's essential for building and maintaining a healthy culture.

HOW LAWYERIST DOES IT: MEETINGS AND COMMUNICATIONS

To build a strong culture and facilitate the flow of information at our business, Lawyerist uses eight distinct types of meetings and communication.

Each mode of communication has a place, a purpose, a goal with a written agenda, and time limits. We know who needs to attend and who will facilitate each meeting, and we have established methods of capturing information, even though we don't take official minutes. Finally, we have a plan for cascading messages that need to be shared with the rest of the organization, as well as a way of capturing important but off-topic ideas that may come up in the course of discussion so we can deal with them later.

Not every firm will need to implement all eight of the following approaches. But they offer a good guide for thinking about how you may approach communications at your firm.

#1. Daily Check-In

This is our version of a daily stand up meeting. Each team member checks in online (we use Slack) and reports on their planned work hours for the day, any big issues they might be facing, deadlines or deliverables the team should know about, and if they need any help with anything.

#2. Weekly Thirty-Minute Check-In

Once a week, the team gathers for a quick check-in. Each person takes a turn sharing personal and professional news from the week, their progress on long-term and quarterly projects, and how their weekly KPIs are performing. This allows us to get to know one another, build trust, and anticipate and troubleshoot potential issues.

#3. Weekly Sixty- to Ninety-Minute Leadership Meeting

During these meetings, we follow a set agenda and walk through how to solve strategic and coordination business challenges in our company. These include HR issues, roadblocks to project completion, or ways we should be coordinating differently to get on the same page.

#4. Weekly Communication of Cascading Messages to the Team at Large

If any information comes out of the leadership team meeting that is useful for the whole company to know, we send out a cascading message to the team. Some weeks, this message isn't needed.

#5. Weekly Team Check-Ins

Once a week, each of the teams in our company (marketing, sales, operations, etc.) have a standing check-in to see how their projects are going.

#6. Ad Hoc Check-Ins

For any ad hoc projects distinct from the regular work of a functional team, those project teams meet with a set agenda around what decisions need to be made and when.

#7. Quarterly Reviews

Once a quarter, everyone on our team has a performance review with their manager.

#8. Quarterly Leadership Off-Site

Once a quarter, we have a leadership team off-site retreat that lasts all day.

KEEPING HOURS IN CHECK

We're all familiar with the term *work-life balance*. We sometimes use it too, but we also acknowledge its limitations. If nothing else, it's misleading, creating a false expectation that everything will always be in equilibrium, which it won't. Further, the very concept starts with the assumption that work and life are in opposition and should be balanced *against* each other.

That said, we get the sentiment, and we certainly support the idea that we should be making time to support our personal lives and goals. Historically, lawyers have treated hard work as a badge of honor. The more they've worked themselves into the ground, the better.

That can't be your goal or the goal of anyone else at your firm.

DROP THE ALWAYS-ON MINDSET

As Stephanie will tell you, she once billed eight hours while on vacation with her three-year-old and husband at Disney World. At the end of the day, her husband turned to her and asked, "Will you ever come on vacation and actually be present with the family?"

That was her wake-up call.

These days, Stephanie works to be intentional with everything she does, whether at work or at home as a mom, wife, and friend. She's constantly reevaluating how she spends her time and asks herself whether she's spending as much time as she wants to spend on each area of her life. If the answer is yes, she feels balanced.

Balance is a relative term. Sometimes, work takes every minute of Stephanie's attention. When she's facilitating Lawyerist's LabCon conference, for instance, she spends little to no time thinking about her family outside of the occasional check-in. For those few days, she is focused on her work and confident that her family is taken care of and happy.

Further, she knows that the conference won't last forever and that she will spend intentional time with her family when she gets home. She may have three dedicated work days every August, but the rest of the year, she has designed her work schedule to be flexible to her needs. If she wants to pick her daughter up from the bus and spend the afternoon in the park, she will.

LIVE YOUR LIFE FIRST

Stephanie loves her job. As a mother, she feels it's important to love her job and spend time doing it. But she also knows it's important to be able to turn that off and tend to the other parts of her life. In fact, if she *doesn't* take enough personal time off, she knows that her teammates at Lawyerist will hold her accountable and remind her to seek balance in her life.

Why do we hold team members accountable for spending too much time at work? First, we believe it's damaging. We've heard too many stories about kids who grew up with absent fathers because their dads were out lawyering and earning $300,000 a year.

That can't be the answer anymore. Work can't be your purpose in life. Life is your purpose in life.

Even for those of you whose work is a huge, important, and motivating factor, there still has to be a life that underpins that work, whether that life involves family time, hobbies, travel, or all three. The law firm you create should support the life you're trying to create.

Second, when you work too much, you're not actually helping anyone. There is a mountain of empirical research to suggest that human beings stop being careful, productive, and clear-headed after around fifty to fifty-five hours of work a week.[18] While this number may vary

---

18 Jon Youshaei. "How Many Hours Is the Optimal Workweek? Fewer Than You Think." Stanford University. May 3, 2016. https://publicpolicy.stanford.edu/news/how-many-hours-optimal-workweek-fewer-you-think

from person to person, and while some people are naturally more hardworking than others, the point remains.

The reality is that the lawyers who are regularly pulling all-nighters or working weekends aren't doing good client work by Sunday afternoon, no matter what they think. That said, we do recognize that circumstances might call for a rare all-nighter. If you have an upcoming trial, for instance, it probably makes sense to stay up late or work a weekend. That's okay. It's not okay, however, to constantly create excuses to work beyond your capacity every week of every month of every year.

ENCOURAGING VACATIONS

In addition to holding yourself to roughly forty hours a week, you need regular sustained breaks away from work. Everyone needs time away to completely shut down. As Stephanie will attest, her best lawyering came after she took an eight-week sabbatical. Everyone around her was shocked that she—the managing partner of a law firm—could possibly take so much time off, but she did it just the same. When she came back, she felt energized and ready to practice law again.

We're huge advocates of all kinds of sabbaticals. In fact, we believe every lawyer should work them into their lives. Lawyers have a rough job; we carry our clients' problems with us everywhere we go. You may not realize it, but your body, brain, and soul need a break. From that perspective, vacations are strategically beneficial.

Again, Stephanie can attest to the importance of well-needed time off. In her career as a lawyer, she took client calls from everywhere imaginable—from a New York City bar to the delivery room after she'd just given birth to her first child. She even came back from maternity leave early for a trial! While in the past, Stephanie might have shared these war stories as a badge of honor, here she shares them as an example of what *not* to do. Everyone needs time to rest, relax, and heal.

CREATE THE POLICY—AND SET THE EXPECTATION

Offer regular time off at your firm—and then create a culture where taking time off is encouraged. Many firms offer vacation benefits, but they either implicitly or explicitly discourage their employees from taking them, usually with some variation of the line that when you're not working, you're not billing.

Firms should abandon such toxic messaging. As we've explored throughout this book, there are plenty of ways to create a viable business that makes money even when the most senior member isn't there. You just have to be clear about what you want out of your life and then design a business that accommodates that.

Besides, to make money in your business, you have to work on your business—and sometimes the best way to work on your business is to not work at all. Everyone needs the opportunity to step back and clear their heads of day-to-day tasks so they can be reenergized and reengaged. When you have the opportunity to sit back and breathe in some fresh, warm, seaside air, for instance, you might realize the big ideas and rededication from your time off are worth way more than the five billable hours you missed that day.

MAKE THE TIME OFF COUNT

When your employees take time off, respect it. Working from the beach is not a vacation. A vacation is real time away, without needing to check your email. Don't reach out and ask them to work.

This is why the systems and procedures we discussed in chapter 10 are so important; they allow you to know what needs to be covered ahead of time when a team member is away. It may take a little extra work to set everything up before your team member heads out, but if you've documented everything correctly and have the right systems in place, everything should run smoothly.

As always, there are some exceptions. Sometimes, circumstances dictate that you have to reach out to a team member on vacation. These should be *actual* emergencies. For instance, if a partner takes time off while one of their cases is pending at the US Supreme Court, they won't want to be bothered for team meetings or other day-to-day work, but they will want to be notified the second their case comes up. In such a case, you will want to establish protocols for reaching out to that person.

CREATE TRUST

At Lawyerist, one of our company's core values is: do great work that supports a great life. This captures the idea that we want people to work hard and produce quality output. Alongside that, we want our employees to have interesting and vibrant lives outside of work.

We talk about this core value a lot. It frequently comes up in quarterly performance reviews. In fact, team members sometimes get worried that someone isn't living that value by working *too hard* and minimizing the interesting things going on in their lives. If this is the case, we actively encourage that person to take time off.

In fact, we encourage everyone to take time off, which is why we offer unlimited vacation time and paid time off (PTO)—and we don't track these hours in any way. Our general expectation is that team members will take two or three weeks off a year. But if they need more time off than that, they're free to take it as long as they get their work done and stay engaged at work.

Obviously, with such an open-ended policy, there is some risk involved—at least theoretically. In practice, we haven't found that to be the case. So far, our policy has worked well for our team. We credit this to two factors: the high level of trust we have built into our culture, and our commitment to hiring the right people who fit our core values.

Without these two factors, we understand that a policy like ours would be hard to implement. If your team has demonstrated that they aren't trustworthy, then it's hard to feel good about offering them unlimited vacation. But if you find your vacation policies are being abused at your firm, your best bet is to solve the trust problem before you solve the vacation problem.

GET A QUICK WIN

Here's an easy way to make sure you are encouraging appropriate time off and vacations for you and your team: ask each person at your firm this week if they have a work-free vacation on their calendar and, if not, encourage them to schedule one. This includes you. Make sure you have some sort of nonweekend, work-free time off on your calendar that you can look forward to.

SUPPORTING SELF-CARE AND WELLNESS

Unfortunately, mental health challenges, addiction, anxiety, and depression are significant challenges in the profession. Part of the reason is that law can be hard and stressful work. Another part is the deeply embedded social and professional notion that mental health challenges and addiction are signs of weakness—and no competitive lawyer should *ever* show weakness.

Such a mindset effectively shuts off the conversation around mental health and wellness. The whole idea, if not taboo, is outright dismissed. Lawyers have to be tough and competitive. If you want to win, you can't be weak and vulnerable. End of debate.

This is the wrong way to think about such a serious problem. That's why it's important that we have frank discussions about mental health and well-being in the legal profession.

THE PROBLEM WITH REPORTING

The current version of the bar exam asks lawyers to disclose any past addiction or mental health issues. Answering this question is somewhat of a catch-22. Some lawyers might fear that if they're honest about their disclosure, their past issues will keep them from practicing.

But if they lie and they're caught, they will also be prevented from practicing.

It's a delicate balancing act. While it's important to protect the public and not have lawyers who could potentially harm clients, it's also important to drop the stigma surrounding mental health and other issues. If a lawyer has disclosed mental health issues, that means they're aware of them and are actively dealing with them. That lawyer could be better fit to practice than someone who doesn't recognize they have an issue or who otherwise isn't dealing with it.

Compounding this issue is the rule that, in some states, there is a duty to report people if they are suspected of suffering from mental health issues or addiction. This duty to report comes from a theoretically good place. Again, it's important to protect people from lawyers or practitioners who might not be able to fully care for themselves. But it essentially amounts to tattling. Instead of receiving help for whatever challenges they may be experiencing, they're punished instead.

Slowly but surely, state bar associations are moving in the right direction on these issues. There are more and more instances of people with addiction issues who have still been admitted to practice, and the profession as a whole is beginning to realize that simply reporting lawyers who are struggling might be counterproductive.

There is still work to be done, though—and you can help.

WHAT YOUR FIRM CAN DO

As the leader of a small firm, you have the opportunity to make sure everyone in the organization is getting the support they need to thrive both as people and as employees. This could relate to vacation time, PTO, and work hours. Or it could also mean making sure people have the external outside resources they need to feel appropriately supported.

Make this support as obvious as you can. Your employee manual, HR policy, or written systems and procedures should explicitly call attention to your firm's support for mental health and well-being. Make it clear that experiencing hardships or challenges is not a sign of weakness or something that your firm will stigmatize. Then spell out exactly how your firm can help.

So how *can* you help? First, create a healthy work environment. There are so many fun ways to approach this:

- Consider what kinds of snacks you offer and whether they support well-being.

- Bring in a yoga instructor to the office.
- Keep some bikes at their office. If anyone wants to go for a bike ride at lunch or in the middle of the day, they're welcome to.
- Bring in financial coaches to help team members come up with their financial plan (financial well-being is mental well-being, too).
- Offer them a list of resources to use in their own time.
- Make it clear that leadership and HR are always available to discuss any serious issues.

Lastly, consider what kinds of afterwork activities you promote. While our team enjoys fancy cocktails as much as anyone, we're also aware that alcoholism and alcohol abuse continue to plague the legal profession. For this reason, find opportunities for lawyers to enjoy time together in ways that aren't based around alcohol. Drinking together isn't the only way to be entertained.

BE A GOOD HUMAN

Your firm is much more likely to thrive in the future if you and your team members are healthy with active and engaging lives outside of work. Make this a reality by promoting a collective focus on long-term goals while making sure that everyone in your firm is reasonably compensated, included, and taken care of.

You need to be a good human and treat everybody else as good humans. While this isn't hard, you do need to be intentional about how you do this. With some good people systems in place at your firm, it can be a place that makes work enjoyable for you and your team.

> **MORE RESOURCES**
>
> We've put together a set of free tools, templates, and worksheets designed to help you with your hiring and team management. You can download them at law-yerist.com/roadmap/resources.

CHAPTER 14

THE FUTURE OF LAW IS YOURS

For over a decade, we have worked with thousands of lawyers across the United States and Canada to create a sustainable future for small-firm law practice. With this book, our goal was to share what we've learned along the way and to offer you a roadmap for making that future a reality in your practice.

We tried to approach this book to be broadly applicable to different practice areas and jurisdictions. Further, we wanted to account for the inevitable changes coming to you through your strategic choices, good or bad luck, disruptive outside forces or normal successes and failures. Finally, we've tried to make this book prescriptive and technical enough to give you a clear path forward, even if you need to continue working hard to find your own solutions.

JOIN YOUR TRIBE TO KEEP IT GOING

We hope that, after reading this book, you not only share our vision for what your small firm can become, but that you feel well-equipped to begin making this vision a reality.

Most lawyers who try to follow our roadmap on their own struggle at first because they haven't thought about how to implement any of these principles before. As you get ready to take your next steps, just remember that you're not alone. We can help.

LAWYERIST PODCAST

Our weekly show *The Lawyerist Podcast* is one of the most-listened-to podcasts in the legal industry and is full of the ideas and people we mentioned throughout this book. Each week, we talk with a lawyer in our community, a leader of the profession, or a business expert about how to succeed as a small-firm lawyer in the face of a changing profession.

You can listen through your favorite podcast app or at lawyerist.com/podcast.

LAWYERIST INSIDER

If you're looking for a supportive community of peers and the additional resources we've offered in this book we invite you to join us as a Lawyerist Insider.

Our Lawyerist Insider community is completely free and offers:

- A private Facebook group of over 1,000 peers at small firms, supporting each other and working with us to improve their work.
- All of the templates, tools, and other resources we've mentioned in this book to help you craft your Small Firm Roadmap.
- A regular email newsletter highlighting other free content and learning opportunities to keep your progress going.
- Ongoing access to the Small Firm Scorecard so you can track your progress in your custom dashboard.
- And more!

You can join Lawyerist Insider for free at lawyerist.com/insider.

LAWYERIST LAB

If you want to take the next step in investing in building

the law firm of the future, and working directly with our team, we invite you to join Lawyerist Lab.

We've created Lawyerist Lab to include everything we can possibly do to help you succeed in your firm goals for the long term, including:

- One-on-one strategy coaching with our team.
- Monthly topical expert workshops from our coaches, legal industry experts, and best-selling business book authors.
- Monthly mastermind groups to share successes with a group of small-firm peers.
- A complete curriculum of dozens of courses and tools to walk you step by step through implementing all of the components in your Small Firm Roadmap when you need them.
- An invitation to our three-day in-person interactive Lawyerist LabCon conference, noted by many legal industry influencers as the best conference for lawyers.
- And more!

Whether what you need to move forward is a clearer first step, someone to hold you accountable, resources and tools to learn what you need to do, or a supportive community of engaged and influential lawyers leading the future of our industry, Lab is designed to give you what you need.

You can learn more about Lawyerist Lab at lawyerist.com/lab.

Whatever your next steps, we hope you'll commit to building a client-centered, data-driven, and future-oriented law firm. Together, we can change the way small firms practice law.

NOW COMES THE FUN PART

Building a successful small firm has the potential to be the most rewarding and fulfilling work of your life. But remember, nobody said it was going to be easy. Charting your own path never is.

For too long, the legal profession has built its firms around lawyers. We strongly believe that the small firm of the future is client-centric and adaptable to a rapidly changing world. Unless we want to disappear in the face of this change, we have to be proactive and resilient to impending disruptions in the way law is practiced.

It's time to rethink legal businesses from the ground up. The small firm of the future is data-enabled and future-oriented. It is clear on its goals, strategy, and business model. It is intentional about how it markets itself, provides services to clients, leverages technology, and focuses on profitability and financial sustainability.

Above all, it is focused on providing not only great legal work but also on providing a great client experience.

Ask yourself, why did you get into the legal profession in the first place? Was it to make a lot of money, or was it to make a difference? What is the change you want to bring to the world, and what makes you uniquely positioned to help bring about this change?

Only you can know the answers to these questions. But once you do, you'll have a powerful tool in your belt that most firms don't have: clarity of purpose and the drive to make a difference. We're excited to see what you're going to build.

ABOUT THE AUTHORS

AARON STREET is the co-founder and CEO of Lawyerist. For the past ten years, he's been leading Lawyerist's business growth and strategy. His career passion is building thriving culture- and impact-driven companies. In addition to his work at Lawyerist, Aaron is an angel investor and advisor in a variety of startups.

He's spent over two decades working at the intersections of law, business, technology, and policy. His prior work includes corporate strategy consulting, launching a law school think tank, work in the US Senate and the White House, and helping to lead companies in the innovation and robotics industries.

Aaron is active in civic leadership and has served on the board of the ABA Legal Technology Resource Center, the State Assembly of the Minnesota State Bar Association, the board of the Hennepin County Bar Association, and as a trustee of the Hennepin County Bar Foundation.

He graduated cum laude from the University of Minnesota Law School with a concentration in international trade law in 2004, where he was an articles editor of the *Minnesota Journal of Global Trade* and the graduate student representative to the University of Minnesota Board of Regents.

He, his wife Kelly, and daughter Mary Lou enjoy solving escape rooms, paddle boarding on Minneapolis lakes, and experimenting with fermentation projects in their kitchen.

SAM GLOVER is the founder of Lawyerist. After starting his own law firm in 2005, he started Lawyerist as a way to share what he learned about law practice and connect with other "similarly different-minded" small-firm owners. Sam is the host of *The Lawyerist Podcast*, the Lawyerist Lens video series, and serves as Lawyerist's chief web developer.

He graduated from the University of Minnesota Law School, where he served as student body president.

Sam has been recognized in the legal community as an ABA Legal Rebel and a member of the Fastcase 50, and his work on the Lawyerist blog has earned it a place on the ABA's Blog 100 Hall of Fame. He has been named a Super Lawyer Rising Star and received the Volunteer Lawyers Network's Volunteer of the Year award.

Sam's volunteering includes the board of directors of HOME Line, a tenant advocacy nonprofit, and Volunteer Lawyers Network, where Sam created an innovative clinic to help defendants in debt collection lawsuits. He previously taught legal writing and oral advocacy as an Adjunct Professor of Law at the University of Minnesota Law School.

Outside of Lawyerist, Sam is a dad, bookworm, and aging skate punk. He also goes camping in the Minnesota wilderness every winter.

STEPHANIE EVERETT leads the Lawyerist community and Lawyerist Lab. She practiced at a big law firm for five years before co-founding her own firm. As the managing partner, Stephanie watched her firm grow from two lawyers to a team of twenty in just seven years.

Her passion for owning and operating a law firm eventually led her to open a consulting practice, where she focused on helping lawyers learn how to run their own firms. From there, working with the State Bar of Georgia, the Georgia Supreme Court, and Georgia's five law schools, Stephanie designed and launched an incubator program called Lawyers for Equal Justice, which was designed to help new lawyers start socially conscious law firms.

Stephanie graduated cum laude from Georgia State University College of Law, where she was the symposium editor of the *Georgia State Law Review*. She is the current treasurer and on the board of directors of the Sigma Sigma Sigma Foundation. She is also a board member and former president of the Georgia State Law Alumni Council. During her career as a lawyer, Stephanie has been recognized as a Rising Star and a Super Lawyer, was named as a top lawyer of the year by *Georgia Legal Trends* magazine, and was a recipient of the Fast Case 50 Award for law and technology.

Stephanie and her husband, Jason, both avid Texas Hold'em players, own a craft beer distributorship, serving the states of Georgia and Alabama. When she's not working, she enjoys spending time with her daughter—as long as it doesn't involve running—in her home city of Atlanta.

MARSHALL LICHTY graduated from the University of Minnesota Law School in 2002 and, in his career as a lawyer, worked at both large and small firms, learning to manage and improve those firms to be more client-centered, tech-enabled, and profitable.

Before joining Lawyerist, Marshall sold his law practice that helped entrepreneurs, startups, and small companies grow and protect their businesses. His passion for educating and advising business owners is what eventually brought him to Lawyerist.

Marshall has served as president of the Hennepin County Bar Foundation, as a member of the University of Minnesota Alumni Association Board of Directors, as a member of the Minneapolis Charter Commission and the St. Anthony Village Planning Commission, and as an adjunct professor at his alma mater, Gustavus Adolphus College.

In his spare time, Marshall hangs out with his wife and two boys, scratches persistent entrepreneurial itches, mentors students and young lawyers, rides his bike year-round, and obsesses over the Minnesota Twins.